THE UNSEEN PRESENCE

One Man's Journey to Freedom

THE UNSEEN PRESENCE

One Man's Journey to Freedom

Mel Goebel

with Nancy S. Caine

Dedication

To my dearest Jane, for reflecting Jesus through unconditional love and gentle strength.

To Nancy, my writer, who by the power of the Holy Spirit brought the testimony of Jesus out through the story of my life.

To Dallen and Glennis Peterson, for the practical ways you show me how to live out my commitments.

To Marv and LaVerne Kinman, for your words of encouragement and support in my early days of release.

To Jim and Mary Beth Vogelzang, for modeling what it means to lose one's life for the sake of gospel.

To Monty and Holly Christensen, for demonstrating God's passion for the lost.

To Jim and Ruth Youngsman, for your godly example of how to be a good steward of God's resources

To my many Christians friends and family who have offered their support along the way.

FOREWORD

The following pages will introduce you to two of the most gracious and giving people you will ever have the privilege of getting to know. Mel and Jane Goebel have overcome overwhelming odds in life and succeeded with tremendous impact on those around them. There will be no doubt in your mind that powerful unseen forces were at work behind the scenes as you read this riveting account of their lives.

It is with great expectancy that Prison Impact Ministries and the *70 x 7 Book Series* presents, *The Unseen Presence*, the story of Mel and Jane. Holly and I will be eternally grateful for their lifelong friendship and willingness to give the inspiration of their lives to countless others by the sharing of their story. We truly believe that this book in the *70 x 7 Book Series* will encourage a powerful and personal discovery for every reader.

All glory, honor, praise and thanksgiving for this book belong to our Lord Jesus Christ.

Monty and Holly Christensen
Founders, Prison Impact Ministries

Chapter One

Running Wild

What makes a twelve-year-old girl slip over the edge, enter a dark moment of the soul, or think that violence will take care of her problems?

I didn't know when I was seven years old, and now, in my fifth decade, I'm not sure I know today. But the clearest memory I hold from the summer of that year is the day my sister Judy took a rifle out of the closet and threatened to kill my Mom's boyfriend.

That dusty summer of 1958 I spent my carefree days away from home as much as possible, growing up outside like some untamed pokeweed. The dirt roads of rural Alabama in the summer were my personal playground, along with meandering brooks and crooked streams that crossed my carefree path. Catapulting down the side of a sun-drenched hill, my twin brother Marvin and I ran freely and surveyed our little kingdom. Out here, with almost-deserted roads and tangled woods, Marv and I created a world of our own, happily away from the noise and chaos found inside our little wood frame home.

In those days, I traveled in a tight pack with Marvin and our six-year-old brother James, also a twin. Hiking through rural Alabama's farmland, full of creeks and mossy ponds, we'd eventually head home, hot and sweaty from the humid summer air. We'd go anywhere outside to escape the stuffy confines of our little three-bedroom house that overflowed with frantic activities of six of seven unruly kids, my Mom and my mostly absent Dad. The house was messy and quarters were pretty cramped. So, outside our one-story home, away from Mom and our sisters, we'd fill the air with the crack and splut sounds of our BB guns, or we'd whittle down dry sticks to use in imaginary swordplay.

It was rare that Mom would interrupt us during our play to draw our attention to other activities. She'd usually be waiting on customers pulled up to Goebel's Grocery, my family's combination gas station/dry goods store attached to our home. The tiny grocery served as a nucleus for rural folks about fifteen miles outside of Decatur, Alabama. It was also the center of our universe.

But not for our parents. Dad drove a truck long distance and was on the road most of the time. When home, he was gruff and often violent. And if Mom was not preoccupied with waiting on grocery customers, then she'd be away from the family when she could, perched somewhere on a bar stool, day or night.

Two sets of small twins basically fended for themselves in those days. Just a few years earlier, four children were in diapers at one time, obviously a strain on the family. Without Dad home much, our life was consistent only in its inconsistency. Were we going to meet the smiling, loving mother in the morning when we woke up? Or were we going to encounter the manipulative, overwhelmed woman who was often consumed with her own pressures? These daily insecurities ate away at our pool of childish strength and devoured our hope.

We all had one thing in common; we shared the pain and shame of the screaming and negativism found in our home. We all heard Dad yelling at Mom, threatening to kill her or us. Like so many alcoholic families, we did our suffering privately, crying into our pillows late at night or escaping into the fields during the day. At nights I would cry and no one would come, and I wondered why no one responded to my loneliness.

In contrast to the life we lived away from our home during the summer of '58, Judy, my oldest sister at home, spent much of her time washing laundry, fixing us meals and trying to bring a sense of order to our home.

But Judy, too, sought escape from our unsettled circumstances. When not busy with us, she fled from her circumstances to her bedroom to read a little book called *The Boxcar Children*. The book tells the story of four orphaned brothers and sisters who suddenly appear in a small town. Led by their thirteen-year-old sister, the children make a home in an abandoned red boxcar they find in the woods. Ambitious, resourceful and away from all adult supervision, they lived by themselves in the boxcar, until they met a crisis they could not handle. The boxcar children learned to overcome obstacles through their own hard work and ingenuity. This was a theme that apparently appealed to Judy.

We hardly paid that much attention to Judy and her feelings of unhappiness. We didn't have much interaction with Mom, either. Maybe we'd listen long enough to give them both a little lip when they wanted us to mind, and then again maybe we wouldn't listen at all. Our summer was lived in search of freedom in the great outdoors. We wanted to soak in all the juices summer had to offer.

Just for fun on slow sultry days, we boys would quietly climb up the rafters of our musty wood barn. Then, whooping and hollering, we'd hang from off the rafters until our arms shook from exhaustion. We'd finally let go and land on unsuspecting pigs below, whose fearful squealing noises always made us laugh as they threw us off onto the dusty barn floor. Rolling in the dirt, pushing and poking the porkers and each other, we'd shriek with delight at our own mischief.

But we really had fun chasing and teasing our fighting roosters during those summers of freedom. Entering their yard, we'd try to sneak up on the biggest of them all, but they always ran when they saw us coming. Feathers and dust flew as we pursued these pranks, happy for the chance to stir up the barnyard. When the frenzied roosters threw their pointy claws at our bare legs, we'd run, laughing hysterically at the commotion we created.

I didn't know it until later, but Judy, like the thirteen-year-old main character in *The Boxcar Children*, planned to rescue us from the life we led. She plotted a move to Nashville, where she, not our alcoholic Mom or our hothead absent father, would help us begin to carve out a new life together.

Not too long before the shrill chirping of the crickets died down for the season, Judy finally put her escape plan in motion. With money saved that she had stolen from Goebel's Grocery, she wanted to set things straight around the house before she left.

It didn't take long for an incident to bubble up that pushed Judy over the edge.

I didn't see how Judy got in the yard with the gun on the day she took matters into her own hands. But what I did see that day made an impression on me that seared a wound in my young soul.

Thomas McAfferty was a man we had seen often around our family grocery store. He'd been hanging around the house, too, and I didn't like it. I'd even asked Mom one time, "How can you do this when Dad is not here?" She flew into a rage and told me to mind my own business, and left it at that.

But that day was different. Instead of quietly letting Mom get distracted with her boyfriend, Judy's boiling point erupted. In her clenched hands Judy held a .22-rifle pointed at the slicked-back black hair of McAfferty.

"Mom, get out of the damn car!" my sister screamed at my mother and the man who was not our father as they sat parked together off our gravel road next to our little grocery store. "And tell him to leave you alone!"

Judy stared at the strange man at the wheel. Motioning with the barrel of the gun, she turned up her volume. "You son of a bitch, get out of here!"

Mom made no effort to move, despite my

sister's furious threats. The dark-haired man, too, was motionless, waiting for Judy to do something.

By this time, four other children had run from the house to the porch, where we watched the scene unfold. Brothers James and Marvin and I huddled close together, knowing something terrible was happening, but unsure about what we were watching.

At first stunned by her daughter's act, Mom finally found her voice. She started screaming back at Judy.

"Get in the house and put that gun up!" Mom yelled out the rolled-down window of the Chevy. "Who do you think you are, telling me what to do, you lousy piece of crap?"

"Leave her alone," Judy told McAfferty. Then, pointing to our mother, she yelled, "Mom, get out of the car! Get out, now!"

My other sister Jackie, age ten, tried to comfort the rest of us on the porch. We had all seen violence before, even in our own home, but we'd never known Judy to touch a gun. Uncertain, confused, we huddled together in a little nucleus of fear. Jan, my six-year-old sister, looked around and ran inside, clearly afraid of Judy's unpredictable behavior.

The black-haired man said nothing. I didn't know exactly what he was doing at our grocery, or why Mom was in the car with him but I recalled

I'd seen him hanging around outside the gas station before. It passed through my mind that Dad would not be happy about him sitting in the car with Mom

A customer drove up to the gas station, and the familiar ring of the pumps reminded us of another world behind us. Whether or not the driver saw the frantic young girl pointing a rifle at a man in our yard, I don't know, but he could have heard our sobs. Upon seeing the customer, Mom pulled herself back to the world at the store. The tension broke. She quickly left the car and walked back to the house, with Judy marching several steps in front of her. We ran off to our rooms with our dog, Rex, whose unconditional love and sloppy licks helped soothe our childish worry.

The dark-haired man never did say a word as he put the car in reverse, pulled out of the driveway and sped down the country road.

※※※

Later that day, Judy gathered us all in a bedroom and spilled her plans.

"I'm getting out of here," she whispered as Mom waited on customers in the grocery. "I read a book that gave me an idea," she said. "I got almost $400 saved, and I'm going to Nashville to get us a place and a job. Then I'll come get you."

Our oldest sister Marlene had already escaped the cycle of abuse and neglect when she got out of the house at sixteen, marrying at her first chance. She had done all right, set out on her own.

So Judy left our house in Decatur the day after the gun incident, running away for a few days up north, until state troopers picked her up. Her thirteen-year-old girlfriend also was taken in by police. Still holding the $400 stolen from the store, the two told the officers they were headed for Nashville. They returned to us a few days later and little was ever said about the incident.

Although my sister was troubled that summer – scared and angry at the world – my life continued on much as before. While racing through the fields, or peeling down the rocky side roads on our junky bicycles during the day, we didn't talk about Judy, or Mom's drinking, or Dad's anger. We just played and tried to think about other things.

But the dangerous reality didn't disappear. Yelling, cursing, drinking. Dad bullying mom. Beatings, threats. Saying things that made us cower. Calling her names that made us ashamed.

Then in the morning, there was a controlled silence. No one mentioned the screaming in the night, or the thuds heard against the wall.

I didn't know how living in a home filled with alcoholism and abuse would sow the deep seeds of guilt, disgrace, loneliness and insecurity that helped shape me into a criminal. But I know one thing now. The shame and heartbreak I felt standing on my porch the day my sister Judy picked up a gun would be my closest companion for years.

Chapter Two

Road to Rebellion

Early morning sunshine created deep shadows on the golden wheat fields as I crept out of our house. While my brothers and sisters watched cartoons and Mom slept off the alcoholic binge of the night before, I ran outside in the field behind our home.

I sat alone. Birds carried on their songs around me. Softly, the wind blew the stalks of grain in a shimmering pattern. I enjoyed being still for a few minutes, feeling warmth in the sun. At seven, I already knew I had to go someplace else outside my house to escape. In the field behind our house, when I was alone, I was unafraid of people hurting me or yelling at me.

After a few moments of rest in the field, I began to relax. I felt something good come over me, a feeling of contentment and warmth. In my childish mind, it seemed like I wasn't really alone. Something was there with me. Something I felt but could not see. I had never had an experience like this before. This invisible Presence wasn't like my Dad's love, or a secure feeling I felt sometimes when Mom tucked me into bed at night. The Presence was much bigger than that.

In the shadow of this Presence, I felt safe and secure. All cares melted away. I knew I would not be harmed.

As quickly as it came, that Presence was gone. I didn't know what it was, or why it came. But something about that experience remained in my mind until I became a grown man and needed answers for my troubled heart.

Stuffed in the bottom of disorganized clothes closets or shoved in the back of the food pantry, Mom would try to hide her stashes of alcohol. I was the one who found many of the empty vodka bottles, discarded – or more likely – forgotten in her favorite spots around the house.

But no one was fooled about Mom's drinking. When Dad was home, he'd question her daily activities, wondering constantly where she was. Finally, he'd catch her in a slip-up. Then there would be the yelling, the anger overflowing to the boiling point. One night I woke up to find him towering over her, thrashing her with the butt of a gun. She yelled out and tried to defend herself, but with little benefit. Known in his family as having a hot temper, Dad struggled and struggled, and then he'd finally blow. He could stand Mom's running around only so long. The tipping point came, then the inevitable scene and a confrontation, where he'd lash out in fury.

While not a large man, Dad seemed to swell up much bigger when he got mad like that. Mom, however, was wasted, barely contained within her own bones. She seemed smaller and defeated the day after those fights.

Then in the morning, we'd eat breakfast with the prolonged silence weighing heavily around us. Nothing really changed for years. This was just the way we lived each day.

The basics necessary for raising children were usually available during my childhood. Our clothes were clean, hot food was on the table on occasion. Sometimes my mother was compassionate and tender with us. Active and busy all her life, she could be funloving and spontaneous. A roof always sheltered our heads. But the chaos caused by her shifting moods and trips into alcoholic irresponsibility turned our house into a bitter place of anxiety and pain. We all lived just for the moment, without thought for each other's feelings or concerns.

It's no wonder we children all suffered as a result of our mother's self-indulgent and troubled behavior and our father's anger. But we responded differently to the problem. Something about my parents' problems made me feel disconnected from the family. I thought they were hypocrites. Wanting us to be good Catholics, to sit quietly in the pews during mass, they thought we could go from the calm of the church sanctuary to the chaos of home and still be all right.

We'd all be forced to stand in our living room together and say the Lord's Prayer on the days she felt it was necessary. The prayer was a kind of form, a way to make us feel better. I can't say that it hurt us, but I don't know that it helped either. As I look back, I think my mother was reaching out for something or Someone. But from a childish view, the religious message was quite confusing. It didn't make sense to go to church and play all holy, then go home and live the way we lived. The abuse and the alcohol didn't stop just because we said a prayer or two. And although I loved my mother, I felt a great deal of anger toward her during my childhood. She wasn't stable, and she left me alone too much, which made me sad and drove me away from the family.

Because I was a shy kid, I tended to be on the lonely side, too. Emotionally, I think I just needed more than my parents were able to give to me, considering their own problems. I drifted and grew up like some tumbleweed on a Colorado plain, never putting down roots of security in my own family. While I really wanted to have a good and loving relationship with my parents, it never seemed to develop. So eventually, like so many kids from troubled homes, I drew support and direction I needed from another place – my friends. As I grew up, my parents' wishes and their oversight of me became just a shadow of a reality on my turned back.

After Judy took up the rifle, it wasn't long before Dad decided we needed a major change, a move away from our present circumstances. He hoped to bring the family back together again. From that day forward, Dad set in his mind that we should move to Nebraska, his home state, and start over. He pursued a job transfer and soon he was at work at a flourmill in Omaha.

Our new house was in Fremont, Nebraska, a modest community dotted with rolling hills and lush farmland on the outskirts of town. Life seemed to stabilize, and although we still found bottles and knew Mom was secretly drinking, some of the boyfriend issues seemed to have gone away. Dad was not driving a truck long distance anymore, so he was home more.

When we started school, my Mom enrolled us in a Catholic grade school and junior high. It was there many of my lifetime problems with school really started to the surface. School had always been a struggle because I didn't feel connected in the classroom. Keeping my focus on long division or the Pilgrims was a weighty task for any teacher. The structured 1950s classroom environment was not a fit for my overactive, highly physical tendencies.

So it was no wonder I exploded when Sister Mary Alice delivered the handwritten note to my messy desk at Holy Name Catholic School where I was a third grader. The nun looked at me curiously for a second, and finally pointed to the door. "Go," she said.

"Oh great. I'm in for it now," I thought as I shuffled down the empty halls toward Father Mark's office. On the way down there, I ran into Marv, who was coming from his homeroom.

"Why were we called to the priest's office?" I asked him. He hunched his shoulders upward and gave me a slightly crooked grin, moving his open hands to show that he wasn't sure, either. What had I done lately to land me in trouble? I couldn't think of any recent problems. And what did this have to do with Marv?

We opened the door to the priest's office,

expecting to see the tall man waiting behind his desk. Instead, we walked in to find all the other Goebel kids lined up in the office in their crisp blue and white uniforms. Father Mark stood with his hands behind his back, his black priest's frock reflecting dark shadows under his eyes. Judy stood at the end. She was followed by the little twins, James and Janice, then Marv and me. Then standing tall was Jackie, always in control.

"You're probably wondering why I brought everyone here," said Father Mark, looking at the row of Goebels fidgeting in his office.

" I talked to your Mom yesterday, "he said. "She's quite concerned about the way you kids have been behaving at home and here," he added. "Let me be straight. Things need to change. I told her I would help her."

Everyone else seemed focused on Father Mark but me. I knew I didn't like this man very much, but he suddenly became even more distasteful.

The priest picked up a brown wooden paddle on the corner of his desk. Of course, we'd already seen it.

"Your Mom tells me you all are unruly at home, and that you don't listen to her. She tells me you don't give her proper respect. I can help her make sure this behavior stops."

Everyone else seemed to be inspecting his or

her shoelaces, but I stared him right in the face. "Your mom wants me to discipline you, so that you'll mind at home," Father Mark said.

I needed to bolt from the room. I was a wild stallion in an enclosed space. But the door was too far away to reach without getting caught. Nervously, I made a pained face at Judy, showing her what I thought of the priest and his little speech.

Judy reached over to calm me, but it was too late.

"You had better not touch me with that or you are going to be dead!" I yelled out to the priest, who looked surprised. Then he pursed his lips and glared at me.

"Shut up, Mel! Just shut up!" Judy said anxiously, pushing me back a little. Marv poked me with his elbow, and gave me a frantic look with his eyes, quietly begging , "Do you want to get us all in more trouble?" My brother didn't like how I was acting one bit.

"You'll be dead! I mean it!" I said, threatening the priest. It didn't seem important that my brothers and sisters had turned on me, but a final threat by the priest saying he would kick me out of school did get my attention.

That temper tantrum earned me an ear-stinging lecture and further pointed threats from the priest. But I didn't care. The man did not lay a hand on any of us, and I felt as if I had helped the family by telling him exactly how I felt. After his talk, we all quietly left the office and went back to class. We were ashamed and angry about what Mom had done.

When Mom picked us up after school that afternoon, time had only strengthened my feelings. "Why did you have Father Mark talk to us today?" I confronted her as soon as I got in the car. "He was so mean!" Then everyone started yelling at once, telling her how I had threatened the priest and made more trouble for everyone. The car ride was chaos. I had caused much of the problem.

Mom didn't need much encouragement after my outburst to tell me exactly how low I had brought the family, and how I would never amount to anything good. Comments that were often heard at home circled back at me again. It was the familiar refrain of "dumb," "stupid," "slow" and "disgrace." Her stinging comments about me rang in my ears all the way home.

I may have earned a tongue-lashing that day I told off Father Mark, but I was sure of one thing: I was right. They were wrong. Both of them were phonies and hypocrites. I wanted nothing to do with people like them.

Chapter Three

Ridge Riders

"Quick! Get the money," I yelled to my buddy Greg as I skittered down the hallways of the convent on the school grounds at Holy Name Catholic School.

"The nun went to the dining hall, so hurry up while she's outta here!"

I dragged my mop with me, so I could look like I really was working if any holy sister happened to catch sight of me in the hall. "I'll watch while you grab the goods!"

Greg jumped from his bathroom cleaning duties, threw down his sponge, and headed for the little room where the sisters kept the glass containers that held hundreds of dollars in change. That change was given by the faithful who thought they were helping the poor. But really, today, they were helping fund our ever-increasing partying needs. After all, we were poor, too.

I was thirteen and the urge to splurge had come upon me in the worst way. My limited attention span, and my lack of concentration on my studies, had earned me more than my share of detentions at the old convent house. When we got in trouble over at Holy Name, it was cleaning duty time at the sisters' bathrooms. Some days we'd mop their hallways, other days we'd dust and wax the heavy wooden furniture in their living quarters. Those punishments were meant to lead us away from our sins.

The way I saw it, however, the church just ripped off people for their money, so I was justified in ripping them off. I'd only take enough for a couple packs of cigarettes, at first. Then Greg and I started partying a little harder, and we found we needed the funds to buy booze for the weekends. We could stuff the bills we needed in our pants pockets, or slip the change in our book bag, without being detected.

Eventually Sister Elizabeth and Sister Mary Ellen found out about our profiting from the poor and notified authorities. We were busted by the church and kicked out of the Catholic school for good. My parents were frustrated with me. They knew I was headed down a wrong road, but I had stopped listening to them by then.

Nothing about school interested me. Every subject was dull and brittle. I cared nothing for reading books or learning science or social studies. Instead, I fiddled in my seat, daydreamed my time away, and as I got older, spent more time thinking about what I would do after school to make myself feel better. Those students who were focused and disciplined seemed like they were from a foreign culture to me.

It wasn't hard to identify other kids who were having the same kind of trouble I had. A "ridge rider," as I called myself, looked for the next adrenaline high, and sought immediate gratification through sex, alcohol and, a few years down the road, drugs of all kinds. By age fifteen I'd gotten heavily into pot, moving on to cocaine, speed and hallucinogens in rapid succession.

We ridge riders would say to each other, "We're in this for life." Our friends took the place of our families. We were drinking and partying hard, talking crazy with each other and thinking we were the center of the universe. Sex provided an emotional escape and we usually had no problem finding teenage girls who were also riding the ridge.

On a misty fall day of my ninth grade year in 1966, I came to the conclusion that my school days were over. I'd already blown off much of the first part of the semester, to make more time for partying. When I was in junior high, parties were pretty much limited to Friday and Saturday nights. Now, at North High School, I moved even further away from any kind of adult control in my life. The parties just went all week.

"Let's do it today," I whispered to my partner Davis as students entered their second period classes. I went to my locker to get the stuff. After the bell rang, I set off to my friend Steve's room, walked into class while the teacher was teaching, and said, "Let's get the hell out of here." The teacher looked at me strangely, saying, " What are you doing? Leave my classroom." And we did.

We repeated the same scene in the classroom of another dude, who got up with us and strode out of class, shooting the teacher an obscene gesture as he left. The whole school scene seemed so foreign and foolish. I definitely was through with school, and obviously I thought the school was going to be finished with me.

Before we all left, however, we planned to give the school a special send-off as only some of its more delinquent members of the school community could. Earlier that week we bought small spray cans of police mace off the black market from a guy who sold us drugs. Then on our last day at school, three of us each chose separate floors of the three-story high school building. Holding the mace close to the floor, we pushed the button on the can, and walked from one end of the hallway to the exit at the other end. Within minutes school administrators set off the fire alarms to get people out of the building. Students started streaming out of the high school, rubbing their eyes. By that time, however, my buddies and I were carefully parked across the street on a curb, laughing at the disturbance we had created as our goodbye initiation. Their trouble was a big joke to us, and we laughed our way through the two hours the students stood in the mist and rain outside the school.

Life, school, adults – they were all one tremendous joke. Whether it was the school send-off, the drugs, or the desire to find my own niche in this crazy rotten world, no matter what the cost, I decided to do things my way.

Chapter Four

Carl Scott, Scapegoat

Bright headlights of the oncoming traffic weighed down my back as I walked down 90th Street in suburban Omaha. The street sounds filled my ears with a dulling roar; darkness engulfed me as I tried to make sense of my surroundings.

Beyond the pain I experienced, I wasn't sure of much else. Three days ago I'd started scoring methamphetamines; there'd been no need to sleep since then. Seventy-two hours of non-stop partying created a throbbing buzz that made me feel jittery and anxious.

Lights and sounds blended into a shadowy foam, as if I was moving around the outskirts of a dream. A restless craziness had overtaken my mind, drifting into a place where there used to be sanity. Traffic noises and swooshing sounds made by the cars as they passed became a backdrop only to my throbbing emptiness.

"I've overdone it," I thought to myself as I walked alone. "I'm over the edge, but what the hell? No one cares anyway." Although I had overdosed before, this was the first time it looked like the road I traveled might have an early ending.

Any fear I felt as I stumbled through the grassy roadside was distant and vague. As the silhouetted figures in the cars came into my blurred vision, an urgent voice in my mind said, "The light will make you free. Go to the light."

I tottered around on the road's edge, unsure of what to do. My life unfolded as one worthless experience after another. I'd never allowed myself to think like this before, but now, with the end in sight, I knew death was truth. Life had lost any meaning. Even being totally loaded – my daily condition for the last three years – didn't dull the depth of this pain. I'd always been in control, or at least too tough to admit when I hurt. But things seemed different. I was an eighteen-year-old loser who was little more than a bundle of nerves. The drugs had stolen what small sliver of good there was left of my life.

"The light will make you feel better. You'll be in a better place. Go to the light," the voice urged me. "Step away from this world."

There was no peace in this life. Maybe there

was a better place in embracing the light, I thought to myself. With just a few small steps, I could end it all and feel better … or at least feel nothing. Either way, relief would overtake emptiness.

"Hey! Do you need a ride?" My daze was broken by the voice of a friend who had seen me while he drove down the road. "Hurry up. Get in," he said through the driver's side window, gesturing for me to jump in.

"I'm hurting," I mumbled to the friend.

"You've been speeding, haven't you?" he asked.

"Yeah," I said. That was all I had to say. He drove me to my apartment where I slept for more than a day. Then I got up and scored some more drugs again. What else was there?

Days and nights were totally switched around for years. I'd go to bed at 5 a.m. and get up in the late afternoon to get high again. Then my buddies and I would snort crystal meth or cocaine, along with the alcohol and pot that we always used before we'd party all night. If we were lucky we'd pick up some women and bring them home for more revelry long after the bars had closed. The next day was a mirror image of the day before.

In the late 1960s, rebellion was in the air. Even in the cornfields of Nebraska, the seeds of societal discontent could be felt. My friends and I felt like society was a legal rip-off; that authority was our main problem. Cynicism reigned, along with drugs.

With my growing addictions consuming my time, there also emerged a corresponding need for cash, which led me to expand my criminal range of activities and skills. From burglaries to auto thefts and drug sales, I further developed my illegal connections. Eventually caught by the law in a few minor scrapes, I always seemed to get out of them relatively unharmed. Ripping people off wasn't all that difficult. My buddies and I became quite good at lifting people's household belongings and shiny new cars.

But a couple of surprise trips to the county jail over a period of months signaled to me a growing need to protect myself against getting busted, big time. If I got picked up again, I'd probably go downstate, to the Nebraska State Penitentiary, where I'd move into the major leagues. Hard time downstate wasn't part of my plan. Since my chances of getting busted were rising alongside my illegal activities, I planned a new strategy. What I needed was a diversion, a foolproof false ID that would help me if things got hot.

Thus, Carl Scott was born. Someone else could take my rap. He was my alias, a scapegoat. It wasn't too hard to get my hands on a blank birth certificate and make it look old. Rubbing fine dirt into the paper yellowed the document and I further wrinkled the certificate for good measure. Then I obtained a Social Security card with my birth certificate. Finally, I took another driver's test and passed under the name of Carl Scott.

My preparations were tested soon enough, as my buddies and I were picked up and hauled to jail, busted on a burglary. Carl Scott was the suspected guilty party.

When I went before the court, I answered to Carl Scott. Since Carl had not been in front of a judge before, he got off almost scot-free; *he* received probation for just two years.

The whole court scene was a joke. As I walked out the door after court, once again a free man, I sneered while I tore up Carl Scott's identification. This was really stupid. Those pigs would never hear from Carl Scott again.

Little did I know God had a plan that mirrored my own desire for someone else to take my pain. But God's chosen Son who took the brunt of my wrongdoing wasn't a figment of my own need for escape – He was Jesus. He was the Son of God who took the weight of sin on Himself for my sake. And He took the pain not just for one rap, but for all my crimes.

Although I didn't know or care much about Jesus, I did know about getting away without paying the price. Being able to con the system was an ability I had developed and improved over time; it was a deeply ingrained part of my nature. After I walked away from court as a free man, I was relieved that I was smart enough to let good old Carl Scott pay the price I never, ever wanted to pay.

Chapter Five

Doing Time

Shackled and handcuffed, I rode in silence in the back of the cruiser with my personal "escorts" who now were taking me to my new home, the Nebraska State Penitentiary. Carl Scott had taken the rap once for me, but it wasn't enough. A drug raid went down on a home where I was living, and narcotic officers nabbed me. There was no way to beat this rap. I was headed to the pen for two to five.

Summer signaled its bounty outside: warm breezes, lush golden wheat fields and green pastures spread before me, but they only reminded me that my freedom was coming quickly to an end. Seated behind the wire mesh cage, I actually cared little for the familiar scenery outside. My thoughts centered on pushing down the fears that lay ahead for my two-year stint at the Lincoln-based state prison.

A strategy for survival began to form in my mind. I would not let anyone dominate me; I would take on anyone who confronted me; I vowed to do anything necessary to survive the inevitable confrontations. Violent men, driven by their own dark demons, would challenge my weaknesses in a culture ruled by strength, manipulation and power. I didn't plan on becoming one of their victims.

As the iron gates opened, a rush of adrenaline signaled danger approaching. Fear left a sour feeling in my stomach.

Now the game had started.

The Nebraska State Penitentiary was a massive concrete structure that looked like a castle from King Arthur's days, only more like a square block. Inside its dark concrete-blocked hallways, a game was played, and I was an unwilling player.

A series of doors and gates opened and shut quickly as I left the familiar world of freedom, now exchanged for a cellblock full of men shuffling in boredom and with egos running wild. I passed through a heavy gate. One closed, another gate locked. A series of guards and keys passed before me. I was hit by the blare coming from radios, heavy gates slamming, whistles, shouts and conversations that echoed around me, I lifted my head for a second to view what was ahead. This human warehouse reflected men of all races, glaring, dozing, sitting on the toilet or holding small mirrors to try to get a clear look at other inmates. The concrete walls did nothing to absorb the noise of the place; the sheer fullness of the sounds coming from a huge stable of angry men took over my senses.

As I moved through the prison intake process, I was handed my new blue denim clothes and my number: 28138.

"Get used to it, kid," said a guard, as he checked me off his list. As if I was a wild animal ready to strike, I glared at the officer, but he did nothing. After all, he'd seen that look on hundreds of faces before.

The cell house, a red brick building with three levels, became my holding point. I was taken to a four-man cell with four bunks, the aisles offering barely enough room to walk between the beds. Disinterested-looking men sat in the cell, bored and sleepy, idly staring at the frightened newcomers who entered their world. A hail of cusswords came flying down from the tier above us. I kept my eyes down and kept my mouth shut.

"Hey, man, what you in for?" asked a man smoking a hand-rolled cigarette.

"Drugs, theft," I said, looking down as I put down my meager belongings. "Got two to five years."

"Well, you're going to love this hell hole," he said with a grin.

That sarcastic inmate became my one-man welcoming committee to prison life. And in just an hour after entering this new existence, I already knew one thing about the hard road ahead – it sucked.

Prison has a certain rhythm. At 6 a.m. a wake-up siren blared through the three-story cell house. At 7 a.m. an officer flipped a switch that automatically unlocked the doors to the four-man cells. First we ate breakfast, then went to our morning shift of "hard labor." Hard labor consisted of pushing a wheelbarrow full of concrete chunks to a grinder that spat out road gravel. In the winter, the work was grueling and monotonous in the frosty Nebraska deep-freeze, while in the summer I liked being outside.

After a morning head-count and lunch, we headed back out for an afternoon shift, hauling the concrete chunks and taking them to the grinder. At twenty years old, with a life of crime and drugs as the highlights on my resume, I made the grand sum of twenty-five cents a day for all that hard work.

Power and turf became the ruling motivations in the joint as I worked to establish my place in the underground network of institutional life. The most powerful inmates ruled the tiers and determined the details of the prison's pecking order in daily life. For instance, inmates with the most clout could keep their radios up the loudest, or could go to the prison commissary first. If the unwritten order was challenged, just a momentary look at a tough inmate could erupt into a life-threatening confrontation involving the sharpened end of a fork.

Inmates quickly learn one fundamental and universal truth about prison life: No man stands alone. Without protection, without homeboys, those men not willing to fight could be subject to sexual intimidation and pressuring. I learned almost instinctively how to avoid dangerous situations and cover my back.

The inmate underground drug network inside the Nebraska State Penitentiary was a lot more developed than I could have imagined from the outside. Thinking I could work out a beneficial way to keep myself entertained, I tried to get assigned to mowing duty, which seemed to be an easier way to contact the outside world. I did get a delivery system worked out once I got on the yard crew. Visitors to inmates would drop a bag of drugs in a ditch outside the prison. One of us on the yard crew would smuggle it in through a checkpoint or tie it to a rock and send it over the fence to a contact on the other side. Obviously, this was a highly risky proposition. We always had to wait until the guard in the tower faced the opposite direction before we hurled our contraband, but other than that, we found it relatively easy to get the dope inside the gate. We also learned it helped to find a friendlier guard who we would get to know. Then, we'd hope he would not pat-search us as vigorously as some of the other guards would.

<hr />

The word got out pretty quickly that the mowing guys had dope. Business was good. My supply source increased as time went on, so it wasn't long before my status within the prison population grew. My ability to get drugs gained me a respect among the leaders of the inmate population. And, to boost my ego and bolster my increasing self-confidence, I also worked at the iron pile weightlifting and I started to bulk up. Five to six days a week I'd pump weights, and then run three to six miles a day. Even though I was not an exceptionally big man, at five-feet eleven-inches, I wanted to be prepared for any kind of confrontation.

During the next few months in prison, my time was filled with just trying to get by. There was no thought of bettering myself; I didn't take any classes or work on furthering my skills in anything.

I just did my time and continued in my addictions. I could have been smart and used the time for something constructive, but I just lived day to day, smoked pot and worked the prison network for my personal gain. Gliding through the system, I remained in pain and ignored options for change.

In time, I did get busted for smuggling pot into the joint and I was dumped in the hole for two weeks. But Rick Sendgraff, my buddy, worked on the plumbing crew, which gave him access to the chambers behind the cellblocks. An opening around the pipe by the toilet was big enough to hold a joint, so he stuffed one in there for me. I was happy to stay loaded in the dark, by myself, totally in isolation. But whether in the dark of the hole, or in the cells by the harsh light of day, I ran from anything or anyone who asked me to face up to the pain I kept on covering.

⚜

I jammed my time. Seventeen months and four days. After staying loaded as much as possible, I was paroled early. Sent out with my box of belongings and $100 gate pay, I was like so many ex-cons leaving prison. I made lots of promises to myself and to my family. Mostly they involved making a change, leaving my troubled old friends behind. If I could just overcome my need for drugs and alcohol, I thought I could leave some old habits behind.

But within seventy-two hours of getting out, I got loaded. Again. I succeeded at what I knew best: escape. The pressures of no job and the sudden reality of having to make my own decisions on the outside quickly altered my resolve to face life without a little help.

The promises quickly dried up. I didn't want to fail, but I did. Like the sun soon bakes off the dew on the Nebraska cornfields, my good intentions came and went quite quickly. Oh, some thoughts about change grew freely, like the newly planted corn in a wet, warm spring. Those plans were full of hope and plenty for a short season. But the heat of hard realities burned the good intentions. Eight months later, after swearing it would never happen to me, I was busted for violating my parole when I traveled outside the county with my girlfriend. We both were high on pot and alcohol, and I was caught when I drove over the middle line without signaling a lane change.

A state trooper saw us weaving down the highway, stopped us, checked my background and eventually clasped the familiar handcuffs on me as I shot him angry looks. Damn! I was headed back to the joint for a simple violation. After a thirty-day trip to the Aurora, Nebraska jail, I was once again doing hard time within the big stone walls of the Nebraska State Penitentiary.

Chapter Six

The Unseen Presence

The iron gates of the Nebraska State
Penitentiary clanged shut again with a harsh
finality. I shifted my weight around and fiddled
with the handcuffs on my wrists as I sat in the
police cruiser. I wasn't going anywhere with ankle
shackles, that's for sure. Guard towers, barbed wire
and stern-faced corrections officers were the
sobering sights I saw from my seat in the car as I
waited to be processed. While they were a
frightening scene the first time I came here a
couple years ago, this prison's terrain was familiar
to me now.

Not a new "fish" walking into the pen, I knew
exactly what to expect this time. Nothing had
changed on the outside of this broken down
building, and in fact, I could say the same thing

about myself. Nothing had changed. Like so many other of the men behind the cold steel bars, I was a two-time loser.

I had managed to stay high most of the time my first trip in. All I could think of was, "Here we go again. I'm not that bad of a person – so how did things end up like this?"

At least I still had some friends here, I thought. That fleeting notion provided little consolation. "This is not much of a life," I grumbled.

My second trip here in 1973 for "rehabilitation" promised no more hope than the first time I did time. On this, my return stint, I hoped to spend my three-year sentence in another drug-induced oblivion. But working out a delivery system wasn't going to be easy. I could only hope I got back on the mowing detail, although I wasn't confident that could be arranged.

"How am I going to get out of this addiction? I like getting high too much," I wondered as the officers pulled me out of the cruiser.

As I shuffled into that fortress-like prison and was shaved, deloused, signed-in and processed for my stay in the intake area, I realized the burden of shame and guilt was a little heavier this time. However, those thoughts were as random as the birds that occasionally circled overhead, and were about as lightweight. Try as I might to fight it, a bleak depression threatened to overwhelm me.

This trip to the state penitentiary, I did notice a new aspect to my "homecoming." Hopelessness stood next to me like a spectator as I made my way through the first day back. I could not shake that feeling that I really was a failure this time.

The guys in the joint snickered each time someone didn't make it on the outside. They made no exceptions for my return eight months after I left.

"Back for another visit, Goebel?" they yelled as I walked down the halls for the first time that day. "Welcome back, dude."

Dave Miller, an inmate who had bounced in and out of institutions his whole life, saw me first as I walked through the courtyard that separated the cell house and the dorm.

"Hey, Goebel. I thought you would never see this place again!" he laughed as he passed me. "You didn't even stay out a year." Actually, many of the men embraced failure as a way of life, being two and three time losers, so there was little surprise when a guy came back.

That week in the chow line, the word spread fast. Lots of inmates asked what happened. All I could say was, "I got busted. I should have been smarter. Too loaded to care." There wasn't much else to say.

On the prison grapevine, my return actually was greeted with a strange sense of elation. The first words out of some of my friends' mouths were, "Hey man, can you get me some stuff? This place has been dry lately." Apparently the prison connection to pot and other drugs had slowed down when I left my post on the yard crew. That was a problem I hoped to solve, and soon.

Negative mental messages came on strong during that time and I felt the pressure to escape the pain.

"I'll find some stuff once I get into the general population," I thought. At least, I hoped so. I didn't know how I would make it here without the drugs. It was hard to face the loneliness that engulfed me at times, not to mention I'd have to do the rest of my five-year sentence. This second time down, I'd be doing hard time, for sure.

It took almost no time to get back in the prison routine. Just a few days into the grind I was back working out, pressing weights, running six miles in the yard and figuring out how to regain my status in the prison.

One day as I was sitting on a bench in the prison yard, thinking about my family and my old friends, I heard a yell from Dave.

"Hey, Mel, a new busload of prisoners is here," he said. I walked over and watched as the new guys stepped off the bus.

"They're just kids," I thought. So naïve about what was ahead.

But one guy's khaki jacket caught my eye. Hand-written in black marker across the back was the slogan, "Smile, Jesus is your friend."

"Geez, is that guy nuts or what?" I thought. "He'll be torn apart in here."

Somehow, that slogan affected me in some odd way. I knew who Jesus was, or who people said he was. I'd been to mass and recited prayers in my living room with my brothers and sisters. But God was something remote, so far away from life here. Jesus was unreal to me.

I was searching for answers and I needed some hope. In my darkest moments I realized I did not know how to change my own life. I'd tried to stay clean for those few months out of prison, and I had managed to shake a few old friends, but finally, I ended up going down for the second time. If there was an answer to my feelings of hopelessness, on this road I was traveling in circles, I didn't know where to find it as I began my second term in the pen.

Later I found that "Jesus freak" in the prison yard. "Tell me what you know about your friend Jesus," I said with a skeptical challenge.

Fred didn't back down. "I'll tell you what," he said, looking me straight in the eye. "Jesus Christ is your friend whether you like Him or not.

He is real and He gives me peace of mind. He'll give you that too, and joy."

Saying nothing, I stared and walked away. Fred obviously had a problem, and religion may have solved some issues for him, but not for me.

Quite unexpectedly, however, his words stayed in my mind. Those words about Jesus being real bothered me. How did Fred know Jesus was real? What did he know that I didn't know?

A few days later, I saw Fred in the cell house. Something in me pushed to find answers to my questions, and Fred listened to them all.

"What about all the suffering in the world?" I asked him. "Why have I had to go through all this pain in my life?" I understood doubt, but knew little of faith.

He had one quick response to all my questions.

"You have to read the Bible and find the answers for yourself," he said. His words were simple and not very satisfying. Quite obviously, Fred didn't know what he was talking about. I'd figure it out myself. So, I borrowed a Bible from a chaplain and went back to my cell to read.

"If I start a new life, who would I be?" I wondered. "If I let go of the anger, what will take its place? What will I be like if I decide to follow this Jesus?" No answers emerged for these questions and others.

"Goebel, what are you doing with that Bible?" scoffed my cellmates a few days later after they saw me reading the book.

Inmates in the two cells next to me began to taunt me. A large muscled prisoner, with angry red eyes, rode my case pretty hard.

"That book is a bunch of bullshit!" he yelled. "Get it out of here!"

The next day, the same inmate took the Bible off my bunk, lit a match and set it on fire outside my cell as the other inmates laughed. Pages burned and smoldered, making a messy fire that attracted plenty of attention.

"That's what I think of this book!" he said as he stamped out the smoking pages. Nobody stopped the red-eyed prisoner; in fact, others enjoyed the show. Or at least they acted like they did.

I let my pride die away like the smoke that drifted out of the cellblock. Not wishing to get into a fight with him, I stayed quiet.

Another Bible came my way a few days later, a gift from the chaplain. Thankfully, no one bothered me again as I struggled to understand its meaning.

Several days later I entered my cell before my cellmates got there. Not fully understanding why the guys were hassling me, I spontaneously prayed, "God, if you are there, I am trying to read your book. But I don't understand it and my cellmates are tormenting me. I ask you to move me from this cell."

With much skepticism and virtually no faith, I then filled out a "kite," which was a request to meet with my counselor. On that paper I asked to move out of my cell. Because of the counselor's heavy caseload, I didn't expect an answer for three weeks or so.

The next day a guard stood outside my cell.

"Goebel, get your stuff. You're moving," he said.

My heart began to pound with excitement, and for the first time in a long time, joy broke through in my heart. "God heard my prayer!" I thought as I hurried to collect my few belongings.

"Officer, where am I moving?" I asked the guard walking beside me.

"To the dorm, Goebel," he said, nonchalantly. While this routine task meant nothing to him, the walk to the dorm was monumental to me.

Putting away my belongings quickly, I then went straight to the chaplain and caught him as he was leaving for the day.

"Hey, chaplain! I asked God to move me two days ago and I got moved to the dorm. Chaplain, God answered my prayer!"

"Young man, God loves you very much," the chaplain replied.

"Well, just maybe He does," I thought to myself. It was a ray of light in my world without brightness.

⁕⁕⁕

Fifteen months after my return to prison, I had gained respect on the premises for my drug contacts and my relationships with some of the lifers. Dave and Rick and I became a threesome in the joint. Rick helped me get drugs and I only got busted once. My two-week sentence in the hole was earned when an officer's search unearthed a quarter pound of marijuana I'd hidden in my pants.

Now I lived in a dorm housing one hundred and fifty men, six cots to a room. In the dorm setup we had a few more freedoms – like no lockdown and no more blaring wake-up sirens. But the room was humid and musty, with water seeping in all over the floor when it rained. The walls sweated moisture and the roof leaked, which surprised no one living there since the building had been condemned twice before. Taking long-handled squeegees, we'd push the standing water in our cells down a flight of stairs and out the door when the floors got too wet to tolerate.

During this time, the stories and letters I read in the Bible began to make some sense to me. Inside my mind was an anticipation of sorts, an unspoken feeling, perhaps even a hope I could not define. This feeling wasn't with me a few months before and I sought consolation in its very presence.

~~~~~~~~~~~~~~~

On March 16, 1975, sunlight streamed into the barred windows of my prison cell. I was awakened early with a heightened sense of awareness, a sense of something ahead. Conscious of a Presence beside my bed, I opened my eyes. A brilliant light penetrated my being. Someone, I knew, was in the room with me, even if this Presence could not be seen by the human eye.

I shook my head and felt indescribable joy because I was in the room with the light. It was like the joy Fred had told me about, but I could not have recognized it if it had not been inside me, as it was now. My cellmates snored on, unaware of a visitor in their midst.

I got up and walked to the tiny sink at the end of the room.

"I'll wake up here in a minute and come to my senses," I thought as I splashed cold water on my face. But it was as if a ticker tape raced through my mind, right in front of my eyes. Its message read, "Today is the day. Today is the day. Today is the day." I could not escape the message that filled my heart.

No one could see the Presence, but there was

definitely something in the room with me. I had a sense that Someone was standing next to me.

Exploding with emotion, I had to get alone.

Walking down the hallway, I stopped to stare out a barred window into the yard. I started talking to God, daring to address Him as my Father. "I know You're here. I sense your Presence with me," I prayed silently. Quickly, I headed down the dorm corridor to the one toilet that offered a shower curtain and a small private space.

Even there I wasn't alone, as the Presence came with me and just grew stronger. It was as if the Father of the Prodigal Son was opening His arms and hugging me. I knew God was real. Weeping on the floor of that little toilet, I cried out a prayer of repentance for my sin and rebellion.

"God, if you can take my life and do something with it, I give it to You," I sobbed in that tiny room.

In those simple surroundings, a love from another world broke through, setting me free. I felt as if someone had handed me my release papers, from the prison I had created for myself. Burdens were lifted and freedom seemed so close. I reached out and accepted my forgiveness.

I stayed in that bathroom a long time. After my cellmates had gone to breakfast, I pulled back the curtain and readied myself to face the world. But I had something to do first.

I walked to another nearby toilet and began to unscrew the two bolts at the base of the ceramic bowl. The marijuana was still there. Slipping it out, I flushed it away. As I rid myself of the drugs, the powerful Presence stayed beside me. I could almost touch this invisible companion.

Now to the chapel. I ran down a set of stairs on the other side of a dark stony corridor. Halfway down the hallway I ran into Dave, who was coming back from breakfast. I grabbed him by the shoulders and began to rattle on wildly, like a man who has seen a ghost.

"Dave, God came to me this morning ... I've given my life to Jesus ... God sent me a Presence, it came into my room ... I don't know what it was but maybe it was an angel ... and I flushed the dope down the toilet."

I was unprepared for Dave's response.

With his back to the cold stone wall, he closed his eyes. His knees buckled and he slid down to the prison floor.

Dave had fainted.

"We live by faith, not by sight." I Cor. 5:7

Chapter Seven

Faith Tested

"Dave, Dave! Come on, get up!" I yelled while yanking Dave up by the armpits. For a moment, all I felt was fear. What if a bull came along? He might think I knocked Dave out. Punching someone was the kind of thing that got you a quick trip to solitary.

Dave came to. "What's going on? What's wrong?" he asked me as he slowly took in his surroundings and got up off the stone floor.

Dave could not answer at first. He tried to tell me about something he saw, but something that was not seen.

"Mel," he said, grabbing my arm, "there's a look on your face. Your eyes. You're different. Mel, you've been with God."

For the next day or two, Dave watched me

closely, but he wasn't quite sure how to act. Though he would not admit to fainting dead away when he saw me, he did spread the word about the flushed pot. That seemed to make a big impact on him; in fact, it was beyond his understanding.

"If you knew you weren't going to smoke the dope, why didn't you just give it to me? Why did you have to flush it down the john?" he asked. Other inmates got mad, too. "Why didn't you at least give it to us?" they said.

Word spread that Goebel was "spun out" (crazy). Goebel was running around the yard, telling people God touched him.

I attracted a lot of attention by flushing the dope. Pot was so valuable in prison that no one would ever offer it free to anyone else except a partner. But after I flushed mine and decided to walk on the path shown to me by God's light, now inmates were saying, "Hey, Goebel, want to get high?" They'd be trying to hand me drugs, just to see what I would do. I never took any.

Dave and I talked for hours. I also talked to Fred, asking him questions. After that experience in the bathroom, things started making more sense.

"Dave," I said at one point. "You know that 'thing' you felt and sensed, but could not see?" Dave nodded. "Well, it's here now. I can't see it either, but it has stayed beside me. Maybe it's an angel. I know for sure it is either an angel or

Jesus."

Later that week, Dave and I sat on the ends of our beds and faced each other while we prayed together. Dave had been down a long road of sin and despair like I had. But that day he decided to let God change his life forever.

Changes in my life were so drastic; people began to notice something had happened to me. With the changes came a new sense of boldness and a desire to reach those who did not know God's love. Above my bed, I dotted the ugly institutional green paint with large pieces of paper on which I'd written out Bible verses like, *"For God so loved that world that He gave his one and only Son, that whoever believes in Him shall not perish but have eternal life." John 3:16*

Not only did I quit buying, selling and using drugs, but also I stopped smoking "germs," (cigarettes) as well. When I walked in the prison yard I'd carry my pocket Bible with me and strike up conversations about God's power to transform a life.

News of the change even filtered into solitary, where Rick was doing time. About three weeks after the Presence visited my cell, I was sitting on a small island of grass in the prison yard reading my Bible, when I saw Rick. He had just been released from lockdown.

Skepticism rose in his voice when he

approached me. "What's this I hear? You're a Jesus freak?" he questioned.

The old Mel would have challenged such a comment, but not anymore. I wanted to set the story straight, no matter how crazy I looked to him.

"Rick, I want to tell you what happened," I said. He looked at me suspiciously.

There out on the prison yard, under a bright spring sun, I told him about the experience I had and the changes in my life. I read him the first verses of the book of John: *"In the beginning was the Word, and the Word was with God ... The light shines in the darkness but the darkness has not understood it ... To those who believed in His name, He gave the right to become children of God." John 1:1,5,12.*

Rick began to cry, saying he had known Jesus when he was younger, but he had not made a full heart commitment to God. Then and there Rick surrendered his heart and determined to make a new start. Along with the Presence that walked with me in the darkness of the prison, I also rejoiced that a wayward brother had returned to the light.

My new strength was tested in the next year. Violence, sexual pressure and the harshness of prison all remained the same. I saw people stabbed with homemade shanks and felt the threats of fear from men who had no conscience. I even was pushed down two flights of stairs during the start of a prison race riot, an event that was a mistake, an inmate told me later.

But that peace that passes all understanding, the love God had shown to me that day in the prison bathroom, stayed with me through the tough months ahead.

Rick, Dave and I gained a new reputation, that of Christian leaders in the darkness of the prison. Our strength in faith was soon to be tested, however, when Rocky came to us for help.

Rocky was an eighteen-year-old inmate who had only been in the pen about two months. One day he stood at my dorm room door and asked if he could talk to me. I didn't know him well, although I had invited him several times to our Bible study.

He quickly explained his situation. When he first came to the pen, he'd accepted a "brick," a carton of cigarettes, from some older, seasoned prisoners – not knowing there could be a price tag on these "gifts." Now, some of the guys wanted to collect their payment in sexual favors. Rocky was scared and wanted advice.

This was a hard situation to figure out. I asked Rocky if we had a little time so we could pray and weigh the alternatives.

Within a day or two, Rick and I and a few other Christian prisoners had scraped together enough money out of our prison wages to buy a brick at the prison commissary.

Then I took action. I went to the gym looking for the leader of that group, a pushy tough guy worth avoiding at all times. We found him, surrounded as usual by four of his loyal gang members, ready to defend their own.

I walked toward them and held out the brick. "Here's the carton of cigarettes Rocky owes you," I said to the leader. "I never collected the two cigarettes of pot you owed me, so the debt is cancelled."

They didn't just smile and say, "Sure, Goebel. Just great." Miffed, they issued a challenge.

"Who do you think you are, telling us what to do?" My interference in the situation broke one of the basic rules of prison life, which was: "Do your own time. Don't mess with my time. Don't tell me what I can do in this prison and what I can't do." While doing my own time, I saw inmates get stabbed for lesser confrontations. But God had changed my outlook and way of thinking.

My heart pounded in my chest, but I didn't back down.

"Because of Christ, Rocky is my brother," I said with a shaky voice. "I have to help him."

I turned my back and walked away, thoroughly expecting to get jumped any second. But I wasn't.

Five minutes later, the leader of the pack found me in the yard, where I was giving a report to Dave and Rick about what had happened. The leader came to me, now surrounded by seven or eight toughs – all egging for a fight.

"Mel, look …" Rick backed up.

He quietly quoted a Scripture: "The servant is not greater than the master." I understood the meaning: If Jesus had been bruised and battered for who He was, then I should be willing to take a beating for my faith.

I knew I had other options. I mentally went through the people who would fight with me and for me.

"OK, Rick, that's great … but if they pull a knife, I'm running toward the gun tower," I thought to myself. Time hung heavily in those seconds.

But no, that was the old Mel thinking. The new Mel stood tall without a clenched heart. When the leader was just a step in front of me, he yelled, " You take me on, Goebel, if you're so bad!" His chin inched closer to my nose.

I looked at him squarely in the eye and called him by name. "Eric, if you were threatened, I would do the same thing for you," I said. "Because of Jesus he's my brother."

With that, Eric turned and walked away, and his homies went away, too.

Dave, Rick and I knew something happened

that day. We had been part of a great scheme of love, an example of God's goodness overcoming evil. Reminded of a Scripture verse that related, I said to Rick and Dave, *"Greater is he that is in (me) than he that is in the world." I John 4:4 KJV*

Rick knew something significant had happened, too.

"That prison angel is still hanging around," he said. I agreed.

For months afterwards, that gang leader neither hassled nor befriended me; in fact, he ignored me. But in time, his hardness waned. Eventually he acknowledged my greetings and would even stop and chat as we passed each other in the yard. The respect I had tried so hard to earn in my old life by acting tough was actually earned by showing love. It was a lesson I'd learn over and over again in my new life.

"So from now on we regard no one from a worldly point of view. Though we once regarded Christ in this way, we do so no longer. Therefore, if anyone is in Christ, he is a new creation; the old has gone, the new has come." I Cor. 5:16-17

Chapter Eight

The Monastery

Although still behind bars, I felt that my spirit was free for the first time in my life. In the months that followed my encounter with the Presence in that prison bathroom, I started experiencing the love of Christ in my life.

I hadn't felt this good in years! The void in my life was now filled. There was a new peace in my heart. I felt secure in my own identity and believed God loved me. As God's child, I felt connected spiritually and believed God was personally interested in me.

With the friendship of other Christian men also behind bars, encouragement from the Bible and the support from men who came to visit us in prison, my life slowly began to change.

"This isn't a prison anymore," I would often

think to myself. "I am in a monastery." In this protected place, my new brothers in the faith and I had time to study the Scriptures and soak up the words of life together. It was a fertile time in my life. There was no high, no drug or any other substance that could replace a living relationship with the God who had created the universe.

Mom and Dad still came to visit and recognized something had happened to me. But they approached my faith with a cautiousness that told me they were not sure what would happen once I left the prison.

"I'll believe it when I see it," seemed to be Dad's approach to my enthusiasm about my new faith. Mom and Dad were no strangers to the concept of "jailhouse religion," those people who made a commitment to Jesus Christ while behind bars, but who returned to their old ways once they were out. But I didn't put myself in that category, because my personal relationship with Jesus invaded every part of my being. I was a sponge that needed living water – the water of life. Just as I once needed drugs to cope with life, now I needed Jesus all the time ... daily, hourly and minute-by-minute.

My brothers and sisters stopped in the joint every now and then and had no hesitance in telling me they were skeptical about my change. They knew the old Mel who lived life in the fast lane.

Real change, from the inside out, seemed like empty words and nothing more.

But all of the visits from the outside world were critical to my growth, as they are to all inmates. One contact Rick made before going to prison turned out to be very instrumental in my life. In his former life, Rick had been friends with a man named Dallen Peterson, president of KAP's Foods. Dallen teamed up with Marv Kinman, also a faithful Christian businessman, to work with men behind bars.

Dallen's first visit to prison came after Rick had sent him numerous letters full of remorse for the lifestyle that landed him in the pen. Dallen and Marv decided to visit Rick and entered the Nebraska State Penitentiary as innocent onlookers that first day. But they left with a new sense of mission – to help struggling men behind bars change their lives.

The first week Marv and Dallen came into the prison to conduct a Bible study, seven guys showed up. The next week, about fifteen came. Then within six months, we had a group of about seventy-five inmates coming every week – in an institution of about 330 men. It was a revival!

During the months following my conversion, my friendship with Rick and Dave grew. Contentment replaced all my former concerns during this time. Before, I spent a lot of mental energy thinking about things I could not control beyond the walls of the prison, like issues involving my old friends and family. Now I was hungry to learn about Jesus, focusing on the human needs within the prison and on lives that were hurting. New men who came to prison would find our little group of believers welcoming them, reaching out and offering to present Christ's love to them.

You never knew when you brought up the Bible and Jesus what a guy might say.

Just like on the outside, people in the joint were all different, too. Some men were highly intelligent, while others were handicapped socially and emotionally. Remorse consumed some men, while others were hardened from their lives of pain and crime. But we saw a common denominator in all the men; they had been spiritually blinded by the king of cons himself – Satan.

Many prisoners had begun their lives like I had, as little boys watching their moms being slammed down to the floor by enraged fathers or boyfriends. Our emotional wounds began early. Little by little, angry children grew up to be dark and hostile men, lashing out in lives of crime and destruction.

Speaking to the men in our Bible studies, I'd say, "Look! You're the one who has been conned! The Bible says in II Cor. 4:4, *'The God of this age has blinded the minds of unbelievers, so they cannot see the light of the Gospel.'* Satan has one goal, men – to see you spend your life in hell. He doesn't want you to really know who this Jesus is. He wants to keep you blinded and in spiritual darkness, and he will use anything – drugs, sex, pride – to keep you in his territory."

"Satan took your pain and used it as a tool to build a case against the God who loves you," I'd say. "In I Peter 5:8, the Bible says, *'Your enemy, the devil, prowls around like a roaring lion looking for someone to devour.'* Men, since you made it to prison, instead of being killed, you need to thank God because Satan had one goal for your life – and that was to take you out!"

One day while walking the yard like I did every day, I saw a guy all inked up (tattooed) who looked like he was down in the dumps. He sat by himself on a wooden bench near the prison yard.

"How long you in for?" I asked after I introduced myself.

"Done six months already. Got another five years to go," the guy said, looking downward.

"Got any family around here?" We always tried to find out if guys had any support system in place when we talked to them.

The air hung in silence. I waited.

"Got a wife and kids … but haven't heard from them at all." It was a statement that needed no explanation. "I don't even know if they have groceries."

I pushed lightly, hoping he would listen for just a few minutes, and told him there was hope in Jesus.

"Listen, man," the inmate said. "I'm not into that religion stuff. I'm no Christian, I don't want it and don't need it."

"Well," I continued, "will you let our group find out about your family? There's a church that might be able to help them and check to see if they are all right." The prisoner looked up, surprised at my offer.

"What do I owe you for that?" he asked, knowing nothing was free in prison. Doubt crossed his face, but his eyes showed the tiniest spark of hope.

"We want to help your family," I said. "Even if you aren't a Christian, that doesn't mean God doesn't love you and love your family."

Through Dallen and Marv's help, the people of their church formed a lifeline in the prison community. That little thread of love wove together men and women on the outside, people who supported the Little Church in Lincoln on the inside. They were our arms in the free world, and we were able to give so much to men inside because of their support and love for us. That week, church members checked on the inmate's family, found out they had no food, and bought groceries for them.

Sometimes men would ask questions like, "If you're so into the Bible, how do you know it's true?" Rather than getting into an argument on religion, one that often ended up going nowhere, I'd point the men back to God.

"If the Bible is true, God will validate it to you, if you seek Him," I'd tell guys in the yard. "Anyone who seeks the truth will find it," I said. "God will speak to you in a way that shows He knows you."

But I would always end up by telling the guys, "Look, I'm just one guy that got out of the darkness. I'm nobody special and you don't have to listen to me. But God will meet you where you are if you let Him," I said. "He will also give you the faith and power to overcome the junk in your life."

Word began to spread throughout the prison that people's needs were being met through the Christian dudes. Some expressed sincere needs, while others thought we were a dating service to match them with a potential girlfriend! Whatever their motive, I was glad to meet them. Some men even confessed later that they came to us with wrong motives but were touched by the power of God's presence and became believers. Not only was our group growing inside the prison, but

Dallen and Marv were expanding their base of support outside the prison walls.

Eventually, about twenty-five couples from the Lutheran church got onto prisoners' visitor lists and began mentoring young Christians inside the prison. As we grew in our faith, we learned how to feel others' pain and respond to their needs. If men were to find any sense of acceptance anywhere, it had to be in the body of Christ. We gladly accepted all men because we knew it was Satan who had deceived the men into handling their pain in an inappropriate manner.

The "monastery" became as comforting as life in the free world, at least for a while. We were making a mess out of the Scriptures, but we were growing! Our interpretations were crazy, but somehow men were being changed from the inside out. Thank the Lord we had the chaplain and people coming in from the outside world to guide us with some wisdom.

But the honeymoon with that growing body of men did not last as long as I had hoped. Our Little Church in Lincoln began to smolder with division. I was afraid the spark might turn into a flame that could not be controlled.

Dallen and Marv came to our Bible study one Friday evening and I could tell something was up. Men were standoffish that night, and sat with their Bible study cliques. Division took the form of guys pushing "favorite doctrines," like a preferred method of baptism, or speaking in tongues, or insisting the Sabbath be celebrated on a certain day.

For example, Randy, a prisoner from Omaha, was of the "full immersion" perspective. "You've gotta be baptized in the Name of Jesus, "he said, "and that means all the way, not a little sprinkle, " he told the group. It was a doctrine he held as a deep truth, but some men found it offensive. It was a turnoff. As leaders, we knew something had to be done because we were getting caught in theological divisions.

Dallen spoke to the guys that Friday about the condition of our church, and the condition of our hearts.

"What I hear is the beauty of the different variations of the Body of Christ," he said. "But what's more important than holding up our particular set of beliefs is that we hold up Jesus, and we look to Him. Also, that we accept one another and love one another," he continued.

"We can all hold our own beliefs as important, but we can't let these beliefs come in to divide us," Dallen said. "We've got to set these things aside and by our love for one another, show men outside this room what God has done through us, through Christ." He asked us all the question: "How can we walk back out on the yard saying we are Christians, when we aren't showing that unifying love to each other in the room?" Most of the guys in the room knew what he shared was true. Over the months, and with a variety of churches now coming into prison on a regular basis, we had moved from excitement about knowing God to a kind of self-centered religion.

As he finished, we committed to focus on Jesus, and turned away from doctrines that could divide us.

"If you have any encouragement," he said, quoting from the book of Philippians, where Paul speaks about division. *"If you have any comfort from his love, any tenderness and compassion, then make my joy complete by being like-minded, having the same love, being in one spirit and purpose. Do nothing out of selfish ambition or vain conceit, but in humility, consider others better than yourselves."* His words were taken to heart all around, and that day, we broke through a dividing barrier to new freedom in unity.

> *"Dear friends, let us love one another, for*
> *love comes from God." I John 4:7*

Chapter Nine

Talking With "The Man"

Before I left the prison in 1976, I had another early morning visitor. The Unseen Presence came again and stood silently at my bedside, this time at 4 a.m. Usually I could sleep through anything in the noisy prison dorm, with wisps of coughs and snoring echoing in the halls, but this night I awoke with a start.

Familiar warmth filled the room. Remembering the sensation I felt when the Presence entered the dorm before, a growing spiritual sensitivity provoked me to awareness.

Maybe I should get out of bed, I thought. For some unknown reason, I was tremendously thirsty, so I shuffled to the drinking fountain at the end of the corridor. The desk there was manned by Officer Powell, a veteran guard, maybe sixty years old.

Reserved, quiet and a by-the-book corrections officer, the six-foot two-inch guard was a man who demanded respect. I never had a habit of getting friendly with guards and tried not to talk to them at all, other than to process routine requests. Prisoners were the "kept," guards were the "keepers." There was no trust between the two groups.

Officer Powell stared into space, hardly aware of my presence, his head propped in his hands. I suddenly felt moved to talk to Officer Powell.

"How are you doing, officer?" I asked. The silent Presence still at my side, I took the liberty of sitting on the side of the desk.

"Not doing too well, Goebel," Officer Powell said. "Troubles at home. My wife is leaving me."

It was obvious he was depressed, and as he began to tell his story, my mind wandered for just a moment.

Flashing back to the first day I entered the prison, I saw myself being administered state-issue prison clothes, handed to me by a strident officer who made sure I knew who was boss. So angry at the world, and chained in both body and spirit during my first trip to the pen, I peered through a tunnel in my life to view that old self as being very far away. The new Mel, one changed from the inside out, could not have imagined ever hearing anything personal from "the man." But here I was, talking to him as if he was a hurting brother. As he rambled about all of his problems, I was unsure of what to do. I had never encountered a situation like this with an officer. I felt helpless. Then suddenly, I blurted out, "Can I pray for you?"

As I asked that question, I momentarily was aware of stepping over a line that could get me in trouble. Officer Powell let his guard down, and to my surprise, he said, "Sure, Goebel."

Shocked by his quick response, I nervously said my first prayer for an officer. "Dear Lord," I began, "I know you can help Officer Powell and his wife. You see their hurting hearts and their pain. I ask you to touch them with your love and peace and let them know how much you love them. Amen."

From brief conversations in the next few weeks, I got the impression Officer Powell and his wife worked things out. "We're talking again. Things are looking better," he said, smiling just a bit. After that hint of hope, I reflected on how God uses His children in little ways, to bring healing, wholeness and direction to confused people. Somehow, even with the clear-cut rules of institutional living separating Officer Powell and me, I had shared in His divine work.

Early in my journey as a Christian, God started breaking my hard heart. I began to learn how to feel the pain of others and respond to their needs.

My divine "appointment" to talk to Officer Powell provides a good example of what God started to do in me. The Holy Spirit heightened my sensitivity toward others; the outcome was a work of God in my life. In my early life I was only hell-bent on doing what felt good to me, no matter what the cost to others; now I could feel God's love in such a way that I hurt when others hurt and I felt moved to carry their burdens.

As I grew in faith, God started to show me His love for all people. He loves correction officers, parole board members, judges, prosecutors, rapists, murderers and adulterers, and that's not the end of the list. God wishes that *none* would perish, but all come to find a right relationship with Him as Creator and Father.

I eventually became aware of ways I could help some of the new guys in prison. Peer pressure ruled so much of life in the joint; we believers behind prison walls began to see how hard it was for some of the men just to come to our Bible studies. New guys often felt conspicuous about merely walking across the yard to the chapel. We believers realized if we came over and met the new guys at the cell house and walked across the yard with them, they would not feel as vulnerable. All the inmates knew if you went in a certain door, you were headed to the chapel and that was seen as a sign of weakness. It was one of Satan's lies.

"Only Chesters (sex offenders) walk through that door," said one inmate about that walkway and door to the chapel. Men incarcerated for sexual crimes, like molesting children, often could not function at all within the prison community and would find their only consolation in the chapel. Prison old-timers, who held much of the power in the institution, and most men in the general population, despised those who had committed sexual crimes. If men were to find any sense of acceptance anywhere, it had to be in the body of Christ. We in the Little Church in Lincoln gladly accepted all men. Their sin was no different than ours.

Over my months in prison, the Unseen Presence, the Holy Spirit, alerted me often to a need. Through my developing relationship with Jesus, I realized God was calling His children, created in His image, into a relationship with Him. While still behind bars, I began to sense my life's calling would be to help people, with God's prompting and His power, no matter who, where or when.

*"My grace is sufficient for you, for my power
is made perfect in weakness." II Cor.12:9*

Chapter Ten

Open Doors

The doors of the "monastery" opened up for me for good on August 21, 1976, as I finished my five-year sentence in the Nebraska State Penitentiary. With my state-issued suit on my back, a few possessions in a box and the second round of $100 gate pay, I was launched back into a world that saw me as a person to be avoided. I was twenty-five years old and a two-time felon.

I, however, had great confidence that my life had been transformed behind bars. I was full of faith, confident that the God who sat as a silent Presence beside my bed in prison would accompany me on the next step of my journey.

Serving Jesus in the Little Church in Lincoln had been my focus for more than a year, and as I got out of prison, I hoped to continue to serve God in the outside world. But as far as getting preparation to re-enter the "real world," well, there wasn't any.

I knew my family would let me stay with them for a short time, but I sensed I could easily wear out my welcome.

Emotions bounced back and forth in those days before my release, from fear to worry and all stages in between. I hadn't had a real job in years. Prior to prison, I didn't work much at all, since I focused on illegal activities. Thus, entering the "real" work force was an adventure. I learned to trust God each day and to pray about practical needs. My faith was a great comfort, as was knowing I had new Christian friends who would give support and help if needed.

Before Christ I would have contacted the old friends who would give me a different level of "support" and "help" if needed, and who also might supply me with ways to mask my pain. But now my faith was helping me face fearful situations I could not have faced before.

That connection a prisoner has to his past is one reason why so many ex-cons end up with a round-trip ticket back to institutional life after just a few months on the outside. Temptations are all around. But I wasn't planning on ever coming back to this place, under any circumstances.

Thankfully, my parents had picked me up at

the prison that August day – which solved my problem of what to do for the first few days after I walked through the prison gate. I had a well-thumbed copy of the King James Version of the Bible in one hand and my few belongings in the other as I hopped into their station wagon, bound for Colorado. In my state of excitement, I thought it was necessary to tell my parents all the details of my spiritual conversion, and of their own need to find the same peace I had found while incarcerated.

"Dad, you've got to get saved, get washed in the blood," I preached from the back seat as we started the trip down I-80 across Nebraska to Colorado." The church you go to is all messed up. You've got to turn from your sin, and give it all to Him." I leaned over the seat in front of me, pointing to the book of John, as my Roman Catholic father grimaced and glanced at my mom. They held their tongues, and withheld open judgment on my Bible thumping that went on for way too long. To their credit, they didn't hurl me out the car that day as my enthusiasm outweighed my wisdom.

"Son, just show me you are a different man," my father finally said after my religious warnings and preaching finally stopped. "I'll believe you've got a changed life when I see how you live on the outside."

Mom agreed. Since I had been in prison, she also had undergone a significant transition of sorts, leaving her alcohol addiction behind. She'd gotten involved in Alcoholics Anonymous, joined a good church, and often told me she'd get down on her knees each day to pray for me while I was in prison. But while my own enthusiasm might have been contagious in prison to the guys seeking answers, it served as little more than an irritant in the enclosed car.

Stopping for a hamburger at some fast food stand along near Grand Island, Nebraska, I saw a pretty girl who smiled as I walked up.

"Nice day out," I said as I admired her outstanding features. I hadn't been with a young woman in a long time and really felt starved for a little female attention.

"You from around here?" she asked.

"No, I'm just traveling across the state to Colorado to see some family ..."

When she walked from the window with my order, I blurted out, "Hey! I might not see you again so I want you to know – God loves you and has a special plan for your life."

To my surprise, she said, "Thank you." I don't know what I expected, but it felt good to see her smile and show acceptance of me. For so many years, reaching a low point in the first few years in prison before my conversion, I saw nothing but rejection from people. My life meant nothing to others, I felt, and I hated the person I was. But now, motivated by the Holy Spirit, I felt everyone needed to know about the price Jesus paid for sin.

"At least someone is listening!" I thought to myself as I walked to the car, looking back at the young woman I wished I could get to know.

While enjoying seeing my family after so many years behind bars, I found the visit to Colorado to be a mixed experience.

"They just aren't understanding," I said to myself after another frustrated attempt to explain to a family member about what Jesus had done for me. My enthusiasm was met with a variety of reactions, ranging from mild indifference to outright scoffing.

At night in bed I began to pray. "Why won't they believe I am telling them the truth?" I wondered. My thoughts shifted to how Satan had blinded me by illusions of this world ... the drugs, the women, the deceptions and stealing. I said a prayer, alone in bed, thanking God that night for His wonderful gifts. And I fervently prayed God would do whatever it took to lead my family to Jesus.

Ex-prisoners have so much going against them, it's a wonder that they ever sort through the details of re-entry into the outside world. Although I had hoped that I would be different, I found myself feeling isolated, angry and uncertain.

After so many decisions are made for you in an institution, you find your life as an ex-prisoner is way too complicated. Simple decisions, such as what to have for breakfast at a restaurant, or choosing clothes or making long distance telephone calls, can cause panic. Many men feel like they have a light flashing in their head that says, "I just got out of prison!" Small relationship problems, or issues involving authority, tend to be exaggerated.

A person who is living as a newly converted Christian in prison may not know how to live for God in the outside world. Already under the burden of having to learn how to adapt on the outside, where he or she was unsuccessful before, a new Christian fresh from prison faces serious obstacles to success. I was no different than the many men and women who are released from prison each day.

I had adapted to prison culture fairly well, even excelling in learning the system and becoming a leader of sorts. But almost every decision was made for me, from what to wear, to what to eat. That structure contrasts with the reality of men and women just out of a correctional institution. Very little structure is in place. There's probably no job, possibly no place to live. Old friends can provoke further problems. The problems are complicated and often spell defeat.

Lucky for me, I did have help on the outside

world. The love shown to me by Dallen and Marv continued when I got out of prison. The Lutheran church that helped me and other men in the Little Church in Lincoln in the prison setting also helped me and others on the outside.

Prison volunteers from the churches rallied around me when I got out and showed me how to get my feet on the ground. Soon after my release, I was living with Marv and his wife LaVerne, in a middle-class home in Omaha. Dallen got me a job and co-signed on a car for me. I didn't know how I would be taken care of, but God provided so many people around me to help. In my case, the hardest part was really figuring out how to live on the outside.

"Man, I feel like I've been away so long," I said to Marv a few nights after moving into his house. "Styles have changed so much in five years! I don't really know what's going on out here," I said. "I'm in culture shock."

"Don't expect it any other way, Mel," he said. "It's going to take time to get settled." And it did.

Everyone on the outside of prison knows most churches meet one hour or so a week. Even though I remembered how things were, I still found that shocking. I wasn't used to so little interaction with other Christians, because in prison, our Little Church in Lincoln met every night for Bible studies or fellowship. Without that daily study and time with other Christians, I started to feel adrift in my faith. How could just one hour a week be "enough?"

"How do Christians make it out here?" I wondered as I walked up to Dallen's doorstep, unannounced, for the second time that week. I was desperate for that sense of structure and belonging I had experienced in prison. I needed every bit of Jesus, every bit of fellowship that I could get my hands on, in order to survive.

As a formerly addicted person, I realized I could not live only having a Sunday worship experience. I had to have Jesus, all day, every day, or I could not manage my life. I was desperate and I knew it.

Dallen and Glennis, always gracious, got used to seeing me hang around their home. Dallen had given me a job driving a long distance truck route for his snack food company, which helped tremendously. He'd also encouraged me to get involved in weekly Bible studies at the Calvary Lutheran Church in Omaha, where I'd been attending. The pastor, Bob Ellison, made a point of telling me I was welcome in his church. I started attending weekly studies there.

"No matter what you have done in this life, this is a place where you can grow," Pastor Ellison told me. "People accept you for what you are and not what your past is like." But even with the weekly studies, I still had trouble figuring out what the heck I was supposed to be doing.

I remember one night of temptation well. While still staying with Marv and LaVerne, an old girlfriend called and asked me to come over. While I knew in my own heart she was interested in more than just a quick visit, I denied my intentions to Marv and LaVerne.

"Don't worry about me," I said as they inquired about the woman. "We'll just laugh over old times and have a little fun." They said nothing. But I found out later, as I walked out the door they fell on their knees and began to pray I would not allow temptation to overtake me.

Driving down the highway to my old girlfriend's house, I started to feel a bit uncomfortable. The feeling grew the further I went. Four or five exits later, I was really feeling pressure. I sensed it was the Holy Spirit convicting me of my motives.

Suddenly, I could go no further. I knew I had reached a turning point. Finding the nearest exit, I turned off on the bridge and circled around, now headed back toward home. As soon as I turned around, that sense of conviction that made me so darned uncomfortable left almost immediately. I exited back into restoration, traveling over the bridge of forgiveness and experienced a peace that passes all understanding. I knew I had done the right thing. It really felt good.

Only when I arrived home did I find out that Marv and LaVerne had stormed the heavens for me that night. It was one of the times I really sensed the power of prayer to convict me of my motives. God was showing me, in this instance and throughout those first few months out of prison, that He could be trusted.

Through Jesus and my new church family, I found the things I needed to help me succeed in my new life on the outside of prison fences. The journey of faith and fellowship, and the challenges of living out my commitments in the body of Christ, provided me the necessary support to live a life free of crime and in obedience to Christ.

> *"But God chose the foolish things of the world to shame the wise; God chose the weak things of the world to shame the strong." I Cor. 1:27*

Chapter Eleven

The Warden's Call

It probably was a stretch for some of those great folks at the Calvary Lutheran Church in Omaha to really accept and love me, but I did feel their love. Pictures I have of myself at that time reflect a rugged-looking man, long hair, dressed in white T-shirts and jeans. For work at the snack food company, my T-shirts and jeans were probably fine. But as far as church in late 1970s went, well, in retrospect I realized I stretched the boundaries of good taste in some people's mind.

However, I knew these good, wholesome church people were touched by my commitment. I think they were intrigued with my focus, and after spending just fifteen minutes in my company, I suspect they could sense my life had been drastically changed by Jesus. I'd spent almost two years on "retreat" in a "monastery," studying God's word and staying in daily fellowship with like-minded men. I was separated from the daily cares of life and was able to focus on what was really important. How many people get to see men's lives transformed right before their eyes? The light of God's grace and mercy shown brightly in that prison, in the darkness of the cold stone cells. I witnessed that light and power of the gospel, living in a situation most people would find deplorable.

As I adjusted to life outside prison walls, I spent more and more time involved in the life of the church. If I wasn't at work, then I plopped myself on the doorstep of Dallen and Glennis or spent time with Marv and LaVerne. Life got easier as the months went by and as I made some Christian friends.

During the fall, I noticed a beautiful dark-haired, shy woman who was the church parish administrator and organist. Through Dallen I got an introduction to Jane Danitschek, who lived on the north side of Omaha and had been working at the church for about a year. A few months later, I found out Jane wanted to go to a Christmas dinner at our church but did not have anyone to take her to the event. Dallen suggested I ask her.

I did call her up the next day and ask her to go with me. Without any other words, Jane simply said, "Yes."

Jane was raised as a pastor's daughter. She was a very traditional and proper young woman. It's hard to imagine her mentally crossing over between dating the man of her dreams ... or me, an ex-con. Picking her up the night of the dinner, I was greeted by her father, a very distinguished white-haired gentleman. We were probably lucky that Pastor Ed Danitschek failed to start on the twenty questions he usually reserved for Jane's male escorts. For that slip, Jane tells me she was very grateful, as she did not know how to explain my five-year stint behind bars.

I got out of her house as quickly as possible and headed for the church dinner.

But after what I considered a nice evening together that December, Jane wasn't exactly looking my way. I'd ask her out again, and without an explanation, she'd just say no. I thought she was being rude.

"Is this how Christians are supposed to act?" I thought, as feelings of rejection began to attack my self-esteem. I took offense at her blunt responses.

At another church function around Valentine's Day, I thought I'd try again. Jane felt it was "safe" enough to go to church events with me, so this time she agreed. We had been involved in a Bible study together, and had gotten to know each other at a distance. Jane observed me and watched how I got along with the group, both as a leader and as a participant, but I don't think she trusted me yet.

Finally, one night after Bible study I asked her out for coffee and to my surprise, she said yes. That night we had a breakthrough, as Jane poured out her heart to me. She told me later she thought I was very gifted at getting someone to speak right to the heart of the issue. I just was surprised she started talking as openly as she did and that someone else saw something special about me. In my own mind, I was still trying to connect the ex-con with a new man I hoped to be in Christ.

From that night on, we became more open to each other, and we eventually became a couple. But there was just one small problem: the very proper Pastor Danitschek did not know my personal history.

Jane asked me not to tell her father and mother about my life of crime, so they could get to know me without my background being a big concern. I hated the thought of the question, "So, son, what have you been doing for the past five years? And where did you go to college?" I was afraid of that moment, and afraid of how they would respond to me. I even thought of lying, saying I had graduated from "Pen" State. But I refused to give in to the temptation of making myself look better than I really was.

God had another plan, one that pushed the

"background issue" way up to the forefront.

People always say God has a sense of humor. I saw evidence of this the day I was scheduled to address a Lutheran pastor's conference meeting. Driving the fifty miles to the conference that day, I prayed and asked God to show me what He wanted me to share with these conservative pastors. My listing that day, on the top of the program at every seat, was, "Mel Goebel, ex-prisoner, tells how Jesus Christ changed his life."

As I walked into the conference room, I thought I saw someone I knew out of the corner of my eye.

There, midway back on the end row, sat Jane's dad.

I admit the thought crossed my mind: "Lord, this sure would be a good time for You to come rescue me." I also wondered if I could suddenly get sick. But my name was in print, and I had already made it to the conference. Claiming sudden illness probably would be a stretch.

I somehow delivered the message to the pastors that I had planned and wondered what Jane's dad would say when he came up to me afterward. To my surprise, he did not talk to me that day, but just mingled with other pastors.

That night at home, however, a conversation did occur between Jane and her father.

"Jane, did you know Mel was in prison?" he

asked.

"Yes," she replied. She looked at his serious face for some hint of rejection or anger.

"You know your backgrounds are very different. You have a college education. What about him?" The answer was obvious.

But that's about all he said. He didn't try and pass judgment, for which I give him great credit, and he did not tell Jane to leave me alone. Jane was very nervous, but Jane's dad appeared to be open. Her mother, Alice, was actually more than accepting of the relationship. Alice radiated with the love of Jesus. I felt assured she accepted me.

After that day, I did go over to Pastor Danitschek's office and tell him, "If you don't want me dating your daughter, I won't." The conversation didn't last long, but he did not ask me to stop dating her. Later Jane told me he said he respected me for being upfront and willing to approach him with a reasonable concern.

When I spoke to Jane's dad that day, he did tell me some news I wasn't expecting, however.

"I don't know what Jane's told you about her health," he began, "but a few years ago she was hospitalized for some strange numbness at the bottom of her feet, and in her hands."

"She's never said anything about it," I admitted.

"Jane made a long trip to pick up her sister at

college, and thought maybe her numbness was caused by being in the car so long. But I think it's more than that," he said.

In fact, a week in the hospital and a bunch of tests had indicated some abnormalities in the spinal fluid. The doctor had apparently not revealed the extent of his concerns to Jane, but he did tell her dad he suspected Multiple Sclerosis.

I didn't know what a diagnosis of MS might have meant to her life and to our lives together that day. I remember being concerned about the news, but seeing Jane's active lifestyle made that far-off possibility seem less of a reality.

Despite our differences in our contrasting backgrounds and real concerns about my future, Jane and I decided to get married.

It was a beautiful summer day when an unusual group gathered to celebrate our union before God. From long-haired ex-prisoners, ordinary church people to prison chaplains, pastors and family members, some three hundred guests packed into the American Lutheran Church that day as God united two people with completely different backgrounds. It was a glorious time seeing God heal some of the broken pieces of my past life through marrying into a whole and happy family.

The day I walked out of prison, I believed I

would never walk back in, with or without a number. I was surprised, then, when after a few months out of prison I started to feel an urge to go back, this time as an ambassador of Jesus. It wasn't a very pleasant thought, actually.

After counseling with Jane, Dallen and other men on the outside I arranged a meeting with Robert Parrot, warden of the Nebraska State Penitentiary. I wanted to talk about my sense that God was calling me back behind prison walls, to work for Him inside the institution.

"Mel, why on earth would you want to come back here?" the warden inquired over a cup of coffee in his office. "You've obviously been making a successful change on the outside. And prison policy discourages ex-inmates from re-entering the prison, under most circumstances."

I picked up the Bible I brought with me that day.

"Warden, I believe God wants me to come in and share what He did with my life," I said. "I want to tell these men that the power that changed me from a person in bondage to a man experiencing freedom can be theirs. The power from God that took hold of my addictions is freely given. Plus, I want to have fellowship with my brothers on the inside."

The warden leaned back in his large leather chair. He seemed touched by my comments, as I wasn't certain he ever encountered a request like mine. Making no commitment, he said he'd think about it.

Two weeks later I was working at the snack food plant and Dallen called me into his office.

"The warden called today and gave you permission to come in for that weekly Bible study," Dallen told me.

I felt my heart jump in my chest. Dallen was excited, too, that I could join him and Marv every week in prison. We joined hands there in his office and thanked God for allowing me to return to prison, the place where he had transformed my life.

It wasn't long before I heard those familiar sounds of prison life behind me: the noises of keys, the closing of steel gates, the sounds of men talking as they waited for their time to run out. As I worked with Marv and Dallen in prison, I eventually stopped thinking about the surroundings and just focused on the message and the men.

"I'm living for the Lord outside prison, guys, and I'm making it. I'm not coming back in with another number," I told them.

It was a hope all men in the room shared, and also reflected an unspoken fear. The concept of "jailhouse religion" loomed over men who had never been successful on the outside before.

From that day on, whether in snow or ice, Marv, Dallen and I visited the little church in prison each week. We'd pray as we drove the hour there and back, and ask God to show us how to impact the staff and the inmates for Him. Often we sensed a sweet Presence fill the car, as there was great joy and singing as we traveled on I-80. We were on a mission together for the God who loved us and had brought us together in His plan ... to be His instruments to reach hurting people in prison.

"The Lord sets prisoners free ..." Psalm 146:7

Chapter Twelve

Jubilee

Jubilee. The name of the newsletter in my hands had a nice ring to it, indicating a time of rejoicing and festivity, a celebration. In the Bible in the year of Jubilee, slaves were set free, and all debts were cancelled. Every seventh year, the Hebrews in the Old Testament celebrated a Year of Jubilee. During the Jubilee, the farmers would not plant crops, and prisoners would be allowed to go free.

I could see some parallels. I was enjoying a year of Jubilee when I got out of prison, knowing my debt had been paid to society. Jesus had cancelled what I owed God for my sin. I rejoiced in my first tastes of true freedom.

The Scripture notes that a Messiah would come to proclaim the message of Jubilee in Isaiah

61:1-3a: *"The Spirit of the Sovereign Lord is on me, because the Lord has anointed me to preach good news to the poor. He has sent me to bind up the brokenhearted, to proclaim freedom for the captives and release from darkness for the prisoners, to proclaim the year of the Lord's favor and the day of vengeance of our God, to comfort all who mourn, and provide for those who grieve in Zion – to bestow on them the crown of beauty instead of ashes, the oil of gladness instead of mourning, and a garment of praise instead of a spirit of despair."*

I looked over that *Jubilee* publication carefully one day in 1979, after Jane's dad showed me one of its articles. The message of hope spoke loudly from those pages. From crime to Christ. From hate to forgiveness. The message that a new life could be granted by God for those behind bars was refreshing and welcome, as was the thought that men and women behind bars could be free from their darkness.

In the *Jubilee* newsletter, the church was shown responding to crime and its victims. The powerful message hit home with me. The publication reflected a deeply held religious conviction that no life is without worth, that the power of Jesus Christ can reform even the most sin-hardened men and women behind bars.

Mary Kay Mahaffey was a good example.

Mary Kay and her husband lived a life much like the notorious Bonnie and Clyde. Married at fifteen to escape an alcoholic father, she drifted from one dead end to another until she married her second husband, Paul, a professional safecracker and gambler. During a burglary she committed along with her husband, a partner tried to cheat Mary Kay out of her share of the take. Her notorious temper got the best of her, and she shot him in the leg, saying, "I'll leave you lying there, bleeding to death, or you can give me the money and we'll get you out of here."

"My only motivations were bitterness and revenge," she said in the *Jubilee* newsletter. "I didn't care about anything else."

Years later, after the FBI cornered her and threw her in jail, words of her Christian mother and Bible stories began to filter back from her childhood. She asked God to change her heart and something happened. A new inner peace replaced bitterness and she stopped her fighting. Eventually, Mary Kay went back to school while in prison, completed her studies and then earned her Master's degree after leaving the institution. Today, Mary Kay serves as a counselor to troubled families outside prison .

Stories like Mary Kay's touched me deeply. Intrigued about how I might fit in such a group, I began to explore the organization publishing the newsletter, a group called Prison Fellowship.

Prison Fellowship is a ministry focused on sharing the gospel message with men and women in prison. The organization was started by Chuck Colson, former special counsel to President Richard Nixon. He's a man who spent time in prison himself. After his own conversion and prison experience, Colson became convinced of the need for the Christian message to be presented to incarcerated men and women. So in 1976, using proceeds from his best-selling book, *Born Again,* Colson started Prison Fellowship. Today, Prison Fellowship programs and volunteers are in hundreds of prisons across the United States and the globe.

Innovative in-prison seminars and Bible studies are conducted to encourage inmates to grow in their faith. The organization also works on issues related to crime, restoration and punishment in the American justice system. Additionally, as one of its more well-known efforts, each year hundreds of thousands of families with incarcerated loved ones are touched through the Angel Tree program. This successful volunteer effort provides Christmas presents to children of inmates. Through Angel Tree, prisoners are able to help strengthen their ties with their children by providing a personal Christmas present for each child.

In *Jubilee* I noticed a core truth I also held:

crime is caused by the lack of moral training during the formative years. The answer to crime is the personal transformation of individuals. Apart from the life-changing power of Jesus Christ, I have seen no program more effective than Prison Fellowship that can lift a person out of a criminal lifestyle and restore him to responsible citizenship.

I was tremendously impressed with Prison Fellowship and wondered what my next step would be. Direction came more quickly than I expected.

While speaking in a Baptist church in Lincoln, Nebraska, a friend of Chuck Colson's, Herb Jost, introduced himself to me.

"Young man, we need you here in Nebraska to promote the ministry of Prison Fellowship," Herb said, after we exchanged greetings.

"I've just become aware of Prison Fellowship," I said, explaining how I had received a copy of the *Jubilee* newsletter and had been visiting the Nebraska State Penitentiary on my own.

A few months later, Dallen and I found ourselves packed up and on a trip to Washington D.C. to meet the vice president of Prison Fellowship, Ralph Veerman, a devoted man of God.

"Mel, what makes you think you can do the job?" Ralph asked me after he'd given me a rundown on the whole organization.

"My life was such a mess when I got to prison," I explained. "Because of what's happened to me, I've really got a passion to tell men and women in prison about Jesus' great love for them. I've totally changed, and I know they can be set free from the inside." I shared my testimony, hoping we were really on the same page about my future.

We ended the meeting on a very positive note, expecting great things ahead. Ralph believed I was the right one for the job. Apparently, so did Chuck Colson. A call from him a few days later welcomed me on board with Prison Fellowship as the Nebraska state director. I could hardly wait to begin sharing with prisoners, and also to tell folks at churches how they personally could get involved helping men and women behind bars.

As the months passed, my ministry really cranked up. I spoke in hundreds of churches across Nebraska and visited all of Nebraska's prisons, jails and youth facilities. There were about 7,000 men and women behind bars in the state. My goal was to build relationships with these men and women so I could expose them to the life-changing power of God's message. And God gave me great favor in Nebraska. To this day there are church people and ex-inmates who became involved during that time and who remain active in prison ministry. They also continue to be special friends today.

⸺⸺⸺⸺

One part of the new job kept me on my knees: trusting God for my financial support. I'd never had to raise money before for my own expenses. To figure out how to approach people with the story of Prison Fellowship was a challenge. Part of my strategy was to speak in churches and tell people how God was moving and changing lives. Also, I spent a lot of time visiting one-on-one with former contributors, asking them to support the Prison Fellowship ministry and me. Every day I asked God to help me get the money together. Often I had little faith.

One of the most unique encounters I had during my Prison Fellowship work in Nebraska occurred soon after I got the job. I had been given a few names of previous donors who might be willing to support the prison ministry, so I made a couple of phone calls. Al and Nadine Peters agreed to meet with me to talk about Prison Fellowship. Although reluctant to ask for money, one day I dressed up in a suit and tie and drove out to a family farm on the plains. Chickens and dogs hugged the fence as I drove up the driveway to the house.

Nadine greeted me at the door, a gracious woman who quickly set me at ease. She ushered me into the farm's pickup and we headed off to the fields. Driving past rows and rows of sun-ripened corn, we made fast tracks until the farmhouse was but a dot behind us. Finally we reached Al, sitting high up in his churning combine, looking straight at the fields ahead of him. Opening the door of the cab, he yelled his greetings down to us, then good-naturedly instructed his wife: "Take that man back to the house and get some real clothes on him!"

We hopped back in the truck and charged back to the farm, where I was suited with more appropriate "laborer clothes," a pair of old jeans and a work shirt. Then, back I went to the fields, with Nadine roaring down the country road. This was a great adventure in fund raising, but even then, I worried a bit. How was I going to ask these strangers for money? The thought of touching on the subject was uncomfortable.

Dust churned up all around the cab, as the massive machine lurched through the fields. With its chains and sprockets rattling and scraping, and the engine roaring constantly, we kind of yelled at each other in the combine.

Without hesitation, this plainspoken farmer dispensed with polite small talk. "Young man, tell me how Jesus Christ has changed your life." Cautiously, I began my story about how God had taken a guy with a screwed up background, given him hope and cleaned him up for His glory.

Somehow, Al was touched by my story and a strong bond of friendship was birthed that day. In fact, both Nadine and Al eventually became my mentors and helped me grow in my faith, in good times and in seasons of doubt.

After opening up my life so completely to this man, I felt a little anxious about how he might view me. I went to bed trying to remember to trust God to supply all my needs. When I woke up that next morning, Nadine told me some good news.

"We're going to give you $1,500 to get you started, and commit to a monthly pledge," she said over a big country breakfast.

God taught me right then and there that He was going to provide for me. I drove down the long farm road with tears running down my face.

"Lord Jesus, forgive me for not trusting You to provide for me." It was a lesson that would take a long time to learn.

As I grew into my new job, God brought people around me to support me in ways that I never imagined or expected. Volunteers, church people and other Prison Fellowship staffers just gathered me in their arms and in their hearts and walked with me as I learned how to be a man of integrity. Several couples, including Dallen and Glennis, Marv and LaVerne, Gordon and Sue Miller and Wayne and Celia Ganow mentored Jane and me during the early months of our ministry and marriage. Not having had the benefit of a loving father in a safe and caring home, I needed "adjustment" in the area of marriage and relationships, for Jane's sake as well as my own. While I grew up not knowing love or acceptance in my family, I now began to feel a great acceptance from all these people who contributed to my success.

Prison chaplains actually offered me some of my greatest training. Dave Traster, the chaplain of the Nebraska Women's Prison, loved me and guided me often through my identity struggles and through my task of carrying a statewide ministry. Chaplain David Cleoter and Chaplain Stuart Firnhaber encouraged me in my spiritual growth. They all accepted me and helped me join them in their ministry inside the prisons where they pastored. I am convinced their impact is why we see revival in our prisons today.

*"Blessed is the man whose sin the Lord will
never count against him." Romans 4:8*

Chapter Thirteen

Pardoned

Jane and I made it a habit to listen to worship and teaching tapes from a variety of ministries as we traveled on vacation. So in 1983 while coming home from Colorado, I popped in a tape of Dr. James Kallas, president of Dana College, for our long drive down I-80. Dana was a Lutheran liberal arts college in Blair, Nebraska.

Jane relaxed and caught up on her sleep while I drove. I focused my mind on what Dr. Kallas had to say about God using Christian colleges to build and develop the gifts and talents of His children. All of a sudden the Presence of the Holy Spirit came over me. It was as if God grabbed my heart and my mind in that car that day, and said, "Go back to school."

That thought, which felt so good at that

second, was soon crowded out with a host of negative messages I'd received while growing up.

"You're too stupid to learn … You're nothing but a failure … You don't even have a high school diploma. What makes you think you could go to college?"

While the negative messages came into my mind with a singular clarity, I knew the source of them now. Satan's dark lies attacked an area in which I felt a lot of insecurity. I rejected the enemy and quoted Scripture back, *"I can do all things through Him who strengthens me."* I fought the negative thoughts and decided to follow the Presence. Driving down the road that afternoon, I settled it in my mind; if God wants me to go back to school, He'll make a way. I know I can trust Him for that.

Academics had never been high on my agenda of things to worry about at any time during my life. I'd never achieved even mild success. Even as an adult I still hated the thought of school. Meditating about my short and unfruitful academic career only reminded me of all the disapproving messages people had given me regarding my lack of intellectual achievement. I'd created havoc at my high school, encouraged others to rebel and follow me in my petty crimes. I did not see how I could continue higher educational pursuits without even a GED.

However, with a sense of prompting from the Presence, I called up the president of Dana College the next week. I made an appointment to meet with him personally, to ask for guidance.

I walked into his plush, formal office and focused on the framed certificates on the walls that detailed his lofty educational achievement Actually, I felt a little sheepish even being there, like a tomcat in a tiger cage. This was a man of studies, someone who seemed to be in a place I knew nothing about. I had completed only eighth grade. His world was foreign to me. My family pattern was to rail against the system and then drop out of it, in favor of earning a degree in "ER," Escaping Reality. I didn't think I had a lot of business being there, but I charged on ahead.

"Dr. Kallas, I was listening to your tapes last week and God spoke to me through your words." He listened intently as I poured out my story.

"I never spent much time in school," I shared, "and the time I spent there was not very productive. I got kicked out of it when I was in ninth grade. Then I spent the next five years involved in a life of crime, drugs and escapism. While in prison I had a huge change of heart, though faith in Jesus Christ. Now, I'm trying to put the pieces back together and live for the Lord."

Dr. Kallas smiled as I continued. "I'm working for Prison Fellowship now, telling men and women how to find freedom from the bondages that put them behind bars. But I sense God was speaking to me through a tape of yours, prompting me to go back to school."

He leaned back in his leather chair, focused on my story.

"Sir, I don't even have a GED. But can you give me advice about where to start?"

His answer was immediate. I was stunned when he said, "Mel, start here next semester."

I could not believe what he was saying. "But, like I said, I don't have my GED and …"

"We'll worry about that later. You just get ready to start here next semester. The details will all fall into place."

I felt like whooping and hollering all over the place when I stepped out of his office, but I kept quiet as this was not the place to yell. Walking across a beautiful tree-lined campus a few minutes later, I started talking to God.

"Dear Lord, I know your Presence has pursued me and your love for me is more than I can understand. You have proven to me that You are real, and I am excited and scared about everything at the same time. Please guide me into this school experience and give me the strength and wisdom to take this step."

That night, Jane and I celebrated together as another piece of my life came into focus, and under the redeeming love of Jesus. God was leading me to conquer one of my biggest fears, school. It was a direction I never would have thought God would take me. It was a harder road to travel, and I always had taken the easy road. But it all made sense. God was giving me strength to conquer the mountains in my life. His Presence was real, for I knew I could not accomplish this journey without Him.

I attended Dana College in 1983, and worked for Prison Fellowship part time. After not sitting in a classroom for years, the adjustment was even harder than expected. Everyone around me was much younger, and I felt self-conscious about my lack of academic skills. I could not take notes very well. My study skills basically did not exist. The subjects being taught did not interest me. The pursuit of a degree seemed fruitless.

"What am I doing here?" I'd ask Jane when school really became a burden. "This is not for me. My retention isn't good and I'll forget all this stuff in a year. What's the use?" She heard these thoughts many times during my college days.

Feelings of insecurity made me very uncomfortable in the classroom situation. In the past, I would have blown up and walked off campus, never to return, when faced with my failures. In fact, through tears and prodding I felt a power in my life that enabled me to go forward to finish my degree in organizational communications from the University of Nebraska in Omaha. It was God's love and presence that helped me accomplish goals for the first time. I had never known a love like this before.

Life was packed to the hilt that year with helping men and women in prison, studying and raising money for Prison Fellowship. Part of my responsibility as the Nebraska Prison Fellowship state director was to help eligible men and women work through the process to receive a pardon. It was in one such circumstance in 1986 that God pushed me in an unusual way.

"Hi Mel!" said the woman's voice on the phone at the state Board of Pardons offices in Lincoln, Nebraska. A cheerful voice greeted me as if she knew me. But I couldn't recall meeting anyone from that office during my time working with the prison ministry.

"Could you help me, please? Andrew Cyrus asked me to call the office to check on the process and time required to for an ex-felon to get a pardon," I said to the woman on the line.

"Honestly, Mel, when are you going to get *your* pardon?" inquired the voice on the end of the phone

Pardon? For me? I had never thought about it.

"How do you know me?" I asked, puzzled at her familiar tone.

"I've seen articles about you in the paper, and

heard about your state work with Prison Fellowship," she said. "So I was wondering when you were going to apply for your pardon?"

In Nebraska, a person must be out of prison for ten years and have a clean record and community support in order to be considered by the Board of Pardons.

On Dec. 12, 1986, two months after that friendly voice suggested I apply for my own pardon, I entered the state capital building in Lincoln, Nebraska. The formal appearance of the state building reminded me of the last time I had entered a courtroom. This time, however, the outcome would be totally different. Walking in the courtroom, I remembered hearing my previous sentence handed down by the judge: "The court finds Melvin R. Goebel guilty of the offense of burglary and sentences you to two to five years hard labor in the Nebraska State Penitentiary." This time entering a courtroom was a reason to rejoice.

Dallen and my wife flanked my sides as the courtroom began to fill up. Members of the Parole Board, the Pardons Board, the Secretary of State Allen J. Beermann and Attorney General Robert M. Spire entered the room. Then everyone stood as Governor Robert Kerrey walked into the room.

All my sin was laid out in front of the court that day. The many acts of burglary, my sentences and my punishments were listed. After I was asked to rise, the governor said, " I have studied your case history since you have left prison and read the letters of support. I've also heard the testimonies of community support on your behalf. By the powers invested in me, the state of Nebraska does hereby grant you a full pardon." My pardon included restoring my rights to bear arms.

My heart beat loudly in my chest at that moment and my throat got tight. Tears flowed freely as I looked around the courtroom at my friends and family who had come to support me. When all my charges were read aloud against me that day, I realized in some small way this is what it must be like on judgment day, when a higher court, with a Most High Judge, will pass sentence on me. How fearful it will be for those who will not be acquitted because they have rejected through sin their pardon offered through Jesus.

Yes, the pardon for my crimes from the state of Nebraska was a great moment. But how much greater was my pardon that day in 1975 when I knelt down in a prison bathroom and let go of my sin, turning it over to Jesus and receiving a pardon for the penalty of all my offenses.

"For He has rescued us from the dominion of darkness and brought us into the kingdom of his Son ... in whom we have redemption, the forgiveness of sins." Col. 1:13, 14

Chapter Fourteen

Rescued from Darkness

As I traveled through the state, speaking in prisons and meeting men and women in their small cells, prison yards and dorms, I saw God do great things. Often I witnessed inmates being set free of all kinds of bondages. Some who were delivered from oppression were those who had served Satan himself, and had been in his army for years. Yet, one encounter with the light, power and love of Jesus Christ brought these men and women running home like the Prodigal Son of the Bible.

One time after speaking at a prison for women, an inmate I did not know approached me. Carol looked lost. I sensed a great deal of anger and bitterness, if not actual demonic activity, at work in her life. Gathering a group of Christian inmates to stand with me, I began to pray for this tormented woman. I asked Jeannie Olsen, who coordinated the prison ministry at my church and who herself was a woman strong in the Spirit, to help me. We began to pray for Carol.

"God, Carol is bound in sin," I said as I watched her face and placed my hand lightly on her back. "She's tormented and in pain. I ask you by the power of Jesus to set her free from all the things that keep her from knowing You!"

We touched her gently, and continued praying for her only for a few minutes or so. Suddenly she pulled away and said, "Stop!"

"I can't take this," Carol said. She was stiff and holding something back. A little confused, I let the matter alone and told Carol I'd be praying for her in the coming days.

The next week, I received a letter from one of the Christian sisters in prison. She said Carol had become sick after I left. Several of the women stood by her bed and prayed for her. Apparently, something had happened. God is in the business of changing people who have participated in deep darkness. Carol was one such person, and she renounced Satan's practices and lies so she could live a new life.

One inmate wrote and told me, "Carol has changed and is now walking around the prison telling everyone that Jesus changed her!" Her story sounded like something right out of the New

Testament. I put the letter down and was moved to tears. The Jesus who met me in prison rescued another life from darkness.

A month later, Jeannie joined me in another visit to the same women's prison. Carol was waiting for us when we arrived and I marveled at the dramatic difference of her face. The peace and joy surrounding her told me her heavy burden had been lifted.

"Thank you for praying for me," Carol said as she grasped my hand. "God touched me and I'm committed to serve Him now." Her eyes filled with tears as she poured out her story. I was amazed at the glow on this woman's face and the change that was so apparent to correctional officers and inmates. Everyone who knew Carol saw that she had been with Jesus. Even the volunteers who came into the women's prison to lead a weekly Bible study noticed a difference. They told me that they had prayed for Carol for more than a year. They rejoiced over the miracle of a changed life, one they saw transformed in front of their eyes.

During my work with Prison Fellowship I often teamed up with Monty Christensen, another ex-prisoner who turned to the Lord after a life of self-destruction and crime. Monty is the head of Prison Impact Ministries in Montana. Men always respond when Monty tells his story, because Monty's life was a series of failures. In his years of running from responsibility, Monty had mouthed many promises he never seemed to keep.

Men in prison understood Monty's problems and felt a shared understanding of the family forces and pain that drove them both to crime. Likewise, Monty connected on a deep personal level with prisoners because he'd taken years to admit his problems and come clean with his life.

Monty and his wife Holly have chronicled their story in the Prison Impact Ministries book *70 x 7 and Beyond*, which details their long spiritual journey. As an outgrowth of our friendship, we discovered we also ministered effectively in prison. We've teamed up to share our lives with thoursands of incarcerated men and women throughout the United States.

I am convinced ex-prisoners have a special calling to reach the men, women and juveniles in our correctional facilities. As ex-prisoners, we have been where these inmates have been. We walked without Jesus, and with Jesus, in these prisons.

One of the times I saw God intervene in prison in a most dramatic way was at the Limon Correctional Facility in Limon, Colorado. The prison is a lonely outpost in the middle of a desolate plain. Blowing grass, tumbleweeds and the barren land only reflect the despair often contained in this 1,000-bed penal institution. Drive about two hours east of Denver, then head off the interstate about three miles, and you're there out in the middle of nowhere. Surrounded by four fences wrapped with razor wire and tiny electric alarms, the medium-security facility has armed guard towers that tip off casual observers that this prison warehoused some dangerous people.

Unfortunately, the Limon Correctional Facility had been wracked with violence, and several inmates had been killed during the 1990s. Lockdowns were routine, and armed conflicts with officers were not uncommon. The prison had opened in the early 1990s and all inmate turf in this modern facility was up for grabs. As inmates resettled and figured out their allegiances in the complex prison social structure, the prison population would flare up every now and then. But one common theme emerged at this facility; Inmates said they felt a heaviness at the institution, and suffered from a tremendous loneliness there. To make matters worse, the prison was isolated from most of the inmates' families, which brought morale way down. These families often could not afford to drive the long distance from their homes in major metropolitan centers to this desolate spot. The lack of family contact was one more cause for problems to brew out there on the wide-open Colorado plain.

My friend Jim Vogelzang, a successful Colorado businessman with a heart for prison ministry, met with me to talk about this situation in August of 1992. Jim and I had started working together after I moved to Colorado to work with Prison Fellowship in that state.

"The situation has gotten really bad," he informed me that day.

What could we do? I had been seeking God about the situation and I felt like He gave me a plan. It was a risky idea, and if it was approved by the highly cautious state corrections officials, we would know God was making a way.

The plan was firm in my mind. "We are going to go into that prison with one hundred volunteers – men, women, young and old – and do sort of a Christian Woodstock, and we'll do it outside," I said. "For three days, we'll have bands, comedians, music, testimonies of ex-prisoners and an altar call. Guys will hear the good news from ex-prisoners."

Jim didn't see things quite the way I did, however. "Mel, that prison is a security risk. It's very controlled. Inmates are never even allowed to walk on the grass, much less sit on it. Plus, officials don't let but one or two pods of inmates out at a time. They never get the men all together at once; it's just not done. You and I both know this is one very tough place."

"I think the Lord will provide a way," I said.

A sense of faith in what God had showed me welled up in me. So soon I got to work at the Colorado Department of Corrections in Colorado Springs. Within two weeks I had a meeting set up with all the highest corrections officials in the state.

On the day we were scheduled to meet with officials, Jim and a couple other men who worked with me in prison ministry gathered together before we made our pitch. We all stood together, heads bowed and holding hands, to ask the Holy Spirit to have His hand on us. Only God could provide a way for this request to be approved.

The presence of the Holy Spirit in that room of corrections officials was almost tangible. Jim later said he could feel the Holy Spirit almost crackle and pop, the feeling was so electric. Hoping for approval, yet expecting a sea of objections, we presented our plans to fifteen men at tables arranged in a horseshoe in a stark meeting room.

Not one prison official spoke against the idea. These officials wanted positive programming in the prisons, and Bob Furlong, the warden, wanted to improve his prison and do something for the inmates. As an Episcopalian, too, he was touched by the power of the Holy Spirit. At the end of forty-five minutes, we walked out of there getting everything we wanted. Furthermore, as a finishing touch on an amazing day, we even got the additional gift of practical support. The man closest to the head of the corrections department took us aside as we left and said, "If there is any red tape you need to cut through, call me and I'll make it happen for you." We were in complete awe of the way God had gone before us.

That's not to say, of course, that everyone was happy about our plans. The officer in charge of prison security was dead set against our weekend. For him, our plans posed a security nightmare, organizing the logistics of dangerous men let loose around one hundred outsiders who were almost totally naïve about what they were doing. In pre-meetings about the prison yard event, this official blew up and told us in salty language the depth of his feelings.

"Listen here Mel, I don't know why this has been approved," he said in an agitated voice. "Damn it, there is going to be a riot and somebody could get hurt."

We recognized his concerns as legitimate. While most of the time, visitors are generally safe in prison because there are stringent rules governing behavior, this was an unprecedented event that opened a Pandora's box of security problems. Warden Furlong, to his credit, never lost his temper in working out the myriad of details regarding security. He did make one thing clear to his disbelieving staff, however. He said: Whatever it takes to make this place safe, do it. We're moving on with the plan.

The next months, I began to strategize how we'd organize our volunteer team. Church folks across Colorado were being recruited and trained for the prison ministry. Their only requirement was a love for the Lord and a commitment to help men come to repentance and follow Jesus. As part of our background work to prepare for the yard event, I often gathered fifteen to twenty-five people in my home to pray.

Two weeks before the yard event, Jim and I were scheduled to meet informally with the prisoners for lunch and to visit the chapel where we would promote our ministry.

While in the chow line, a beefy ex-biker, maybe six-foot three inches or so, stared me down. Tatted up and down with both amateurish and professional body artwork, Wolfgang showed a steely toughness reflected in the coldness of his eyes. This dangerous inmate had been the bodyguard of one of California's most famous prisoners, Ricardo Narvan, who had killed a security guard in a bank holdup. Ricardo, Jim told me later, was without a doubt the scariest man he had ever met in his years of visiting prisons, hands down. Constantly concealing his eyes behind dark sunglasses, Ricardo wore a blue stocking cap pulled low over his ears. Mean, intolerant, but highly intelligent, Ricardo was known within the prison as someone you did not want to cross unless you wanted a shank in the belly. Now, both Wolfgang and Ricardo were doing time at Limon.

In his pre-prison life, Wolfgang never would have been expected to end up in a criminal's world. He had trained as a Navy Seal and was tougher than some rock washed up on the California shore. I later learned after his stint in the service he attended San Diego State University, where he began his life of crime and drug abuse. Then, the veteran underwent some kind negative personal transformation and decided to work using his abilities for the Hell's Angels. Within this violent biker's community he put his high-level "security skills" to use in "enforcing" the wishes of Ricardo.

Wolfgang recently had done time in California. Then on the day of his release he was picked up by Colorado authorities on a rape charge. This dominating ex-biker, whose scraggly beard hung down to the middle of his chest, watched me everywhere I went before lunch. This one bad dude was none too happy to see me.

Aware of his stare-down, I just played it casually.

"Hey, how ya doing?" I asked the big guy while waiting in the chow line. He looked away, acting like he'd wish I'd disappear.

"Mind if I sit down and have lunch with you?" I asked.

"I guess it's all right," the gruff prisoner replied, not meeting my eyes.

Right then and there the Spirit of God gave me the privilege of seeing into this man's heart. I told Wolfgang that I had done time, too.

"You did time in prison?" he asked, as a hint of openness began to appear on his face.

"Yep. I did two stints in the Nebraska State Penitentiary. Been out a quite a while." Wolfgang then started talking to me. We connected on the inmate level, and he knew I was just like him.

Over our meal we talked about Harley Davidson motorcycles, and what it was like to run with the Hell's Angels. All that tough pretense somehow melted away. After lunch, I invited Wolfgang to come to chapel that night where I would speak. I told him I'd be looking for him.

Interested inmates gathered in the chapel that evening to hear about the plans for the upcoming program. One inmate grabbed my shoulder before I started speaking and said, "Hey, Wolfgang told me to tell you he's outside waiting for you."

A bit startled, I grabbed Jim and we went out to see Wolfgang. Something must be up. The three of us sat down together.

"Hey, man. I want what you got," he said. "I'm tired of living life behind these walls. I'm getting old," Wolfgang said. His request for help was almost a demand. "I don't know how to get whatever it is you got, but I want it."

In a small circle formed with the three of us, we bowed our heads and prayed for Wolfgang, who turned his life around that night. If Wolfgang's sudden change of heart was any indication, we sensed God was going to do great things at the Limon facility in the upcoming weeks.

> *"I am not ashamed of the gospel, because it*
> *is the power of God for the salvation of*
> *everyone who believes." Rom. 1:16*

Chapter Fifteen

Dark Clouds over Limon

The entire prison ministry team knew we were headed into choppy waters when we imagined ourselves sitting on an expanse of grass, awash in a sea of convicted murderers, rapists and criminals of all mentalities. Darkness of the heart and spirit had dominated the atmosphere of this institution, one of the toughest in Colorado. Christians from a variety of backgrounds gathered in Limon to confront this darkness through the power of Jesus Christ.

As we drove to the facility that afternoon, the weather seemed to reflect the spiritual darkness inside the institution. As we came off the freeway and headed down the last few miles toward the facility, we could not ignore the huge black thundercloud positioned right over the building.

Crackling snake lightning centered over the Limon prison like an electric beam shining directly on the institution. Blustery winds blew the tumbleweeds around the plains, as hail popped against the roof of the car. Finally, our driver could not see five feet in front of him and we pulled off the road. The weather just would not let up.

Quietly bowing right there on the side of the road, we prayed. Within a short time the hail stopped and the rain seemed to be restrained. All the while, clouds hung menacingly as before. It was as if some unseen hand was holding back the power that threw those lightning bolts to the ground. The somber black clouds never did go away the whole weekend, but there was no rain at all after our prayer during those three days.

Curious inmates milled around, watching the preparations and sensing something big was about to happen. Excited volunteers waited in the visitors' room. Security teams readied their positions around the yard and on the guard towers.

As the Christian rock band began to crank up their music, the heavy gray clouds parted and a bright ray of sunshine ripped through the overcast sky, landing right on the stage. Men in the yard were just stunned, as I was. As I look back on the videotape, the incident almost seems unreal, like a celestial sign written into an overly dramatic fiction book. Then, as a final touch to this moment, a double rainbow appeared in the distance. God was there to sign His name.

～～～～～

There was no small effort made to keep Limon safe during that weekend. A group of facility guards wearing SWAT uniforms silhouetted the roofs of the prison. Firm-jawed men armed with M16 rifles purposed to keep the peace as they positioned themselves around the yard, tear gas canisters flanking their side. Everyone was committed to making sure nothing got out of hand.

Every prison has its own official and unofficial network of communication between prisoners and the corrections staff. So, before the event, the warden had sent out a few messages through his inmate sources.

One message was: If anything happens, in any way, there will never be another special event like this again. To support the warden's order, we found out later that the older cons had put the word out, too, telling the guys through their network: "If you screw this up, you'll live to regret it." Everyone had a stake in keeping the peace, because if anything happened, visitation rights at the prison could easily be reduced to almost nothing. Thankfully, the men heard the message and counted the cost. There were no incidents during the outreach event.

Included in our weekend presentation was a two-man white rap group, which always drew a lot of response. Other entertainment included a Christian comedian and musicians, plus a group of ex-prisoners who were scheduled to share their stories. Our volunteer team consisting of regular church folks provided the interpersonal part of the weekend.

The interior yard of the prison was about the size of a football field, surrounded by the walls of the prison units. Our plan was to allow men to walk around in the yard and sit in small groups for counseling and ministry after the speakers shared their stories.

Prisoner turnout was fantastic the first night, with about half of the prison's inmates attending the rally. Groups of three to five men informally gathered with a volunteer or two as they sat and talked together in small groups on the grass. As the event progressed, we all sensed the institution's heaviness begin to lift, and by the end of the second day, we all felt spiritual darkness begin to dissolve.

One dramatic story remains in my mind today. Jim served as emcee for the program, introducing the speakers and entertainment. During his free time off stage, he mingled with men sitting on the grass. During one part of the rally, Jim got so caught up in conversation he realized he was going to miss his cue to introduce the next act, so he started to run toward the stage.

Springing to his feet from a sitting position, a blue-clad inmate charged after Jim and tackled him straight to the ground. Startled, Jim pulled himself up and looked at the inmate who had pulled him down.

"Listen, man, if you run around this place, you get a bullet in the back," the inmate explained. "Running gets the attention of those dudes up there on those rooftops," he said as he pointed, "and they'll take you down in less than a second." Shaken but grateful, Jim assured everyone within earshot he had been amply warned about running and would never run again.

Wolfgang found me in the in the middle of the crush of prisoners and shared what had happened in the two weeks since he'd prayed with us.

"I'm still struggling to read the Bible, and man, I'm having trouble dealing with the bulls," Wolfgang said to me after one of the sessions. "But God is helping me do better."

At the altar call, men wept and knelt in the grass. Confessing their sins to each other and to the volunteers, I watched as many as one hundred guys give their lives to Jesus Christ that exciting weekend. That was about one-tenth of the inmate population. To this very day, the warden, inmates and guards say there are men walking around with Bibles in their hands, now committed to Jesus

Christ, who started their journey of faith that day. The warden told me that event changed the spirit of his institution, and it's never been the same.

Ministry did not stop after our visit to Limon, either. Jim and his wife, Mary Beth, heard the heartbreaking stories about how inmates' family ties were shriveling up because they could not afford to visit this remote location. Those of us who have worked in prison ministries see how the families suffer alongside their loved ones in prison.

Instead of just being observers of the pain however, the Vogelzangs decided to help. They teamed up with the Church in the City in Denver, Colorado, and bought several vans to transport these families to various correctional facilities throughout Colorado. The Barn-A-Bus outreach now operates five vehicles that transport prisoner's families each Friday and Saturday to correctional institutions all over Colorado. One of those vans is named after me and sports my prison number: 28138. My name is not on a building, but on the side of a van that takes families of prisoners to visit their loved ones. I count that a high privilege!

Whether we worked in a tough prison like Limon, or a juvenile detention center in a small town, we still relied on God every time we met with men and women in prison. A hunger for

God's will, and for His people, put us in the right place at the right time. Time and again, we saw people transformed from darkness to light by his grace. We saw Jesus in the lives of inmates ready to carry His message of light to their fellow prisoners.

"And we know that in all things God works for the good of those who love him, who have been called according to his purpose." Romans 8:28

Chapter Sixteen

Jane

"Mel, come here. Look at this." Jane said to me one day in 1986 while sitting on our bed. "I'm dragging my left leg. I can't move it the way I want to."

Try as we might, we could not explain the loss of control in her lower left leg. I pushed on her foot; then we shook her leg and she felt nothing different. There was no reason we knew of that would explain this phenomenon. We just hoped the problem would go away. As she stood up, it was clear something was wrong, as her leg now dragged limply as she walked.

We saw her dad later that day and he urged us to get Jane back into the neurologist's office where she had been tested about ten years before. Although we were aware through the years of different symptoms, we had no idea they could be related. Over the years we'd been married she'd had virtually no disability. Jane led an active life. She was an accomplished organist, walked two miles a day, rode her bike and climbed mountains in Colorado at different times throughout those years. Yes, she had experienced a few vision problems, and some numbness and weakness, but we were not sure any of those issues were related.

"I don't want the doctor to throw me in the hospital again," Jane said to me the day of her doctor's appointment. The last time she had visited the doctor, she ended up spending a week in the hospital. Setting fears aside however, she went to her appointment, where the doctor tested her muscle strength. A few minutes later in his office he told her his findings.

"Mrs. Goebel, ten years ago we felt you probably had Multiple Sclerosis, but due to the nature of the disease, it's hard to predict early on. Today, however, I would confirm that diagnosis. We're going to get you started on a steroid, Prednisone, which could clear up your symptoms."

The doctor gave a rundown of the disease and what we could expect: This mysterious condition could come and go for years, causing times of strength and times of weakness. It usually strikes women from ages twenty to thirty-five, but could strike anyone from about age fifteen through fifty. MS is a disease of the central nervous system in which the covering of the nerves (the myelin sheath) is destroyed in the brain and spinal cord. Symptoms include feeling tired, which is sometimes overwhelming, loss of muscle control, numbness, slurred speech, loss of memory, paralysis and loss of coordination. In Jane's case, it took ten years for a diagnosis to emerge, which her doctor said is a common occurrence.

While Jane's dad had told me of a possible MS diagnosis before Jane and I married, we still were stunned by the news. Yet, oddly enough it was a relief for Jane to now put a specific name on what was wrong with her.

Thankfully, just a few days after starting the Prednisone, Jane's disturbing problems with her left leg cleared up.

"This is a miracle drug for me!" she said a few mornings later as she was getting dressed. Jane started writing in her journal during that season, to help her settle her thoughts. She wrote things like, *"Well, I've lived with this for ten years already and it has not impacted my life too significantly. I'm not afraid because I'm going to trust God for the future. His grace will be sufficient."*

We were both so unaware then about what MS really could do to impact our lives. We just had no idea of the devastation it could cause. Over the years, the disease has changed our lives in a tremendous way, which would be obvious to anyone we met.

Jane had periods of strength and weakness years after her initial diagnosis, only to begin to use a cane in 1990. Teasing Jane then, I told her she used her cane more like a walking stick, swinging it around on her arm. We bought a scooter in 1993 but she really did not need it most of the time. After the cane came the forearm crutches. Then a walker. Finally, Jane could no longer stand up on her own, and she settled into using a wheelchair all the time. In 1999, she still drove with help from the hand controls on our van, but unfortunately soon was too weak to drive at all.

In her journal, she wrote, *"It meant a great loss of independence for me to not be able to drive, because I'm a very independent person."*

There has been much loss since the 1970s when her first symptoms were noticed, and although God's grace has been sufficient, it has not always been easy.

Today, Jane's caregiver helps Jane with grooming and household chores for most of the week and I help with dressing and meals. I even put on her makeup, but the eyeliner isn't always straight. In the midst of physical limitations, however, Jane's ministry to her caregivers and other shines brightly. Jane has shared her faith and her life with her caregivers, and some have started to attend church as a result of her expression of her love for God.

From Jane's quiet witness and devotion to the Lord and her decision to trust Him in the valleys as well as on the mountaintops, I've learned so much. She's shown me that no matter what impacts our lives, God can work all things for the good for those who love Him.

> *"We are therefore Christ's ambassadors, as though God were making his appeal through us. We implore you on Christ's behalf: Be reconciled to God." II Cor. 5:20*

Chapter Seventeen

Road to Manila

Canon City, Colorado, is a small Rocky Mountain city known for its spectacular Royal Gorge, and also home to the highest suspension bridge in the world. Towering more than 1,000 feet above the raging waters of the Arkansas River, the Royal Gorge Bridge gives visitors a bird's eye view of twelve miles of railroad tracks running through the Royal Gorge Route. From all accounts, whether traveling through the area by foot, cable car, train or incline railway, the views of this rugged area are spectacular.

A view of the area seen by plane, however, shows more than just the beauty of the majestic mountains and Royal Gorge. Canon City, Colorado, is known for its dozen prisons located at the base of a mountain. Its history as a community is closely tied to the prisons, and today, Canon City serves as home for the Colorado Territorial Prison Museum and Park. Displayed in the museum are unusual artifacts like the actual hangman's noose of the last man executed by hanging in Colorado, an elaborate display of creative confiscated inmate weapons, and one very morbid lethal gas chamber.

Although appreciative of the beauty surrounding Canon City, the area attracted my attention for other reasons. For me, Canon City was a mission field of hurting people locked up in wide range of correctional facilities – from maximum security to one of the largest federal prisons in the United States.

My own view behind bars was so much different than the sight these inmates saw as they gazed out on the free world. While I had looked at the bleak, barren cornfields of Nebraska during the winter and dreamt of a life outside, these prisoners saw the thin razor wire that kept them from the bold beauty of the Colorado Rockies.

After I was appointed state director of Prison Fellowship in Colorado, I often had a chance to visit the prisons of Canon City. They were just a piece of the 14,000 incarcerated men and women who were my responsibility in Prison Fellowship. It was a privilege to be God's representative in this prison community, telling men and women how to unchain the shackles around their hearts caused by sin. Jesus set me free and I knew God held the key to the chains around their hearts. I was on a mission of extending forgiveness, love and grace.

Frank is a typical example of the hurting men we faced each day in our Prison Fellowship work. Frank was a very clean-cut inmate at the Fremont Correctional Facility, serving time for armed robbery. His muscular arms and broad shoulders reflected the amount of disciplined time he spent at the iron pile lifting weights. The chaplain at Fremont had called me to support Frank, who fell into a depression after learning of the sudden death of his mother.

While the church and chaplain on the inside of the prison walls serve many of the needs of prisoners, visits from the outside are always coveted. Frank hugged me warmly as I entered the chapel that day. He was hungry for comfort.

"I knew you would come and see me," Frank said to me. "Thanks."

I remembered how much it meant to get a visitor. The death of a loved one while in prison often could send inmates into a downward spiral, like receiving another sentence of despair.

This kind of interaction was a ministry I had often undertaken, both as a prisoner and then with Prison Fellowship. Many times I had counseled other inmates who had lost a parent or whose wife or girlfriend had left them for another man. Generally, most inmates did not have supportive people in their lives who believed in them. Suffering the losses that came with incarceration, whether by death or by disconnection, was a common, painful experience. Inmates confided they had no reason to live when their main, or perhaps only, connection to the outside world suddenly died or decided to discontinue the relationship.

When I got the call from the chaplain, I immediately remembered Frank. Frank's life had been turned upside down by Jesus when I spoke at that prison a year before. Frank belonged to the little church in prison and needed a friend. It was my "job" to offer encouragement and I loved it.

Frank and I sat together, quietly talking about his concerns. Then we shared a moment of prayer. Frank started to weep and the burdens of his loss just seemed to rise off of him. I knew the Holy Spirit ministered to Frank that day.

Back on the interstate on my way to Colorado Springs, my cell phone rang. Myles Fish, vice president of field operations for Prison Fellowship, greeted me with an unmistakable excitement.

"I've got big news," he began. "Listen, Prison Fellowship International is hosting an international meeting in Manila and they want you to come share about prison aftercare! What do you say?"

"There will be people there from about eighty countries who work in prison ministry. We'll have an interpreter to translate for you," he said.

"Think you can get it together in ten days?"

Just ten days? I didn't know if the logistics of getting a passport and everything else would be possible, but I told Myles I would talk to Jane and call him later. Jane was excited, like I was, and believed God was in the trip. We were surprised how quickly the plans came together and in two days I had my passport and plane tickets.

But the trip reinforced a spiritual truth that has stayed with me ever since then: A hunger for God will put us in the right place.

When we seek God, and trust Him in all our ways, God will direct our steps. He also will arrange the circumstances for His own purposes. This trip was a case in point. Along the way, so many "divine encounters" occurred that showed me God put me in the right place for proclaiming His message.

My trip took me from Colorado through Los Angeles, then on to South Korea and finally to Manila. Sitting in the seat next to me on the Los Angeles to South Korea leg of the trip was an immaculately dressed Korean woman. We began with the usual chitchat and eventually she asked me why I was going to Manila. I told her I worked for a ministry that worked with men and women in prison.

"Are you a Christian?" she probed.

I shared with her for a minute or two, and then we sat in silence for a long time, with the woman staring out the window. About six hours into the flight I took out my Bible and a pad of paper and began to read and make notes for my talk. A few hours out from Korea she turned to me and said, "I know this might sound strange, but would you pray for me?"

I felt a certain tingle, identifying it as the presence of the Holy Spirit, and I said, "Sure, I would love to pray for you. Would you mind if I touched the palm of your hand?" I always liked to touch people when I prayed for them and did not feel it was inappropriate to put my finger into the palm of her opened hand. She placed her hand over the seat and I began to pray," Oh God of Abraham, Isaac and Jacob, hear this prayer for your daughter now." All of a sudden this woman began to weep as she started telling God of her sorrow for her sins.

"Forgive me for making education my God and for leading my husband out of a Bible-believing church. And for all the things I have done wrong these past ten years," she prayed. "It's all been so futile."

I removed my hand and she quietly cried for a long time. Once she regained her composure she shared with me that she was a professor at UC

Berkeley and she had replaced her faith in God with her intellectual pursuits, eventually leaving her faith.

"What do I tell my husband?" she asked near the end of our conversation.

"Tell him the truth," I advised. "That you repented of your sins and you need his forgiveness for leading him out of the church. Tell him you want to return to your faith and walk in relationship with the God who loves you." We parted soon after, with the professor thanking me for our talk.

This was just the first of what turned out to be days and nights full of ministry in Manila, much of it focused on repentance. And just like the professor who had a change of heart, much of it seemed divinely connected to the message of forgiveness and change.

Although I was at the conference to talk about prison aftercare, most of the real time of ministry occurred after the talks and was unrelated to the topic at hand. One conference attendee came up to me to share about the burden of his alcohol problem. Another woman, from Africa, poured out her heart about her son, whose life was being threatened by rebels in her country. The needs of these men and women connected to prison ministry were tremendous.

The day after I spoke, three video crew members from the Philippines kept looking at me in the lobby. I motioned with my hand for them to come over to visit.

"We really liked what you shared last night," one man said.

"Do you know Jesus personally?" I asked them. They acknowledged they had attended church as young boys, but nothing else. So I began to pray for them and right there, in the hotel lobby, the three young men began to ask God to forgive them of their sins and put them on the right track.

God kept me busy sharing and praying for people during that seven-day trip in Manila. And while the topic might have been "prison aftercare," for me, the theme of the conference was: If we are hungry for God and if we obey Him, He'll put us in the right place. Our lives will be linked with other searching people, not by a rope of sand, but twined together with the power of the Holy Spirit and eternal spiritual truth.

"Your eyes are like a window for your body."
Matt 6:22, Contemporary English Version

Chapter Eighteen

Window King

Did you know God is in the window cleaning business? I didn't either, until a few years ago.

My window cleaning journey begins simply on a day in 1997 when I overheard a stranger talking about a need they had for someone to wash their windows. Like so many ideas, this one started with a small seed that lay dormant for months before it sprouted wings.

"My windows are so dirty, I ought to go into the window cleaning business," I heard the stranger say as I walked out of a restaurant that day. As the go-getter type, first in my criminal "career" and later in prison ministry, I appreciated what it might take to own my own business. I knew I would enjoy marketing an idea and building a business into something successful. My hope was to channel much of the proceeds of my own business into ministry opportunities for incarcerated men and women. As I was driving home that day, I could not get window cleaning out of my mind.

Frankly, however, I doubt if I had ever cleaned more than a couple windows in my entire life. Cleaning was not an avocation or interest; I was interested in helping men and women get clean from sin, yes. But cleaning windows? Can't recall a serious thought about anything remotely connected to the subject in all my years.

I never had owned a squeegee. Plus, my fear of heights was well-grounded after a nasty fall from a roof. Generally, I tried to excuse myself from any work involving altitude, ladders or anything not connected directly to dear old Mother Earth.

The next day after the window washing comment, I prepared to fly to Miami to address a group of one hundred fifty prison aftercare volunteers. My paper and pen were out on the plane flight as I readied to make notes for the event, when a Scripture popped into my mind. It was Matthew 6:22. The verse said, "*Your eyes are like a window of your body.*" (Contemporary English Version) I read the text and the thoughts began to freely flow.

"God is in the window cleaning business," came the thought. "He desires to clean up the windows of our souls. He is in the business of taking the specks of sin off the windows, and away from our souls, so that we experience more light and peace." Then I wrote down a list of specks of sins that rob us of the light within. Specks were issues like greed, lust, gossip and lack of unity. A little slogan also came to mind: "We bring clarity to your vision." I wrote that down, too.

In Miami, I gathered with an inner-city audience – Hispanics, African-Americans, Anglos and Asians – who had committed their time and energy that day to learn about integrating ex-prisoners into their own churches.

"How many of you know God is in the window cleaning business?" I began as I stood in front of the audience. A few folks in the pews smiled. Some shifted in their seats and looked at me with curiosity.

"We are going to get into training here today on prison ministry in a minute," I said. "But before we do, I want to remind you: God is in the business of cleaning you up. God loves you so much that He desires to clean up any hint of spiritual darkness. In return He fills you with more of His joy, peace, love, and light. As a result, you will experience more clarity in all aspects of your life."

A few heads nodded in agreement. "God loves you so much, He wants you to be full of light. He's come to take the specks of darkness out of your life. The dirt of greed, lust, judgment, lack of forgiveness, bitterness and control can be cleansed from the window of your soul."

Within thirty minutes of sharing a message of hope with these future prison ministry partners, the sweet presence of the Holy Spirit started to work around the room. Holiness filled the place, and people got down on the floor and on their knees to repent.

Let me tell you, friends, repentance is not a Mel Goebel thing. I've never had anybody get down on the floor weeping or crying out to God like people did this day. I've never seen a move of repentance like this in my entire ministry, and I've spoken in a lot of places. That day, miracles were happening as something of God blew in the doors of that old inner-city church.

As I headed back home on the airplane, my seatmate asked me what I did for a living. "I work for a large prison ministry," I said, explaining the purpose of Prison Fellowship and how God had changed my life while I was a prisoner.

Part way into the conversation I was interrupted by a gentle tap on the shoulder. The lady in the seat behind me had been listening to our conversation and said she had something she wanted to share with me.

"I'm sorry to bother you," she said, "but are you a Christian?" She told me she was returning from a women's retreat. At the retreat, a specific

Scripture had been impressed upon her mind and heart, but she thought maybe it was for her husband. Now, she told me, she believed it was for me.

"Please write it down for me," I said, craning to make eye contact with her.

The text she handed to me was Rev. 3:8. It said, "*I know your deeds. See, I have placed before you an open door that no one can shut. I know that you have little strength, but you have kept my word and have not denied my name.*"

The message hit me like a thunderclap; I felt its truth immediately. I thanked the woman for being obedient to her faith in Christ. Maybe God was saying something about making a drastic change from prison ministry into window cleaning? It was definitely not a thought that I manufactured myself.

Back home, the theme of "window cleaning" seemed to be everywhere. One of the first "honey-dos" out of Jane's mouth when I returned from my trip was to "have the windows cleaned before my mom and dad get here." She had never asked me to wash windows before, but I agreed to get it done. After looking through the ads in the phone book, I settled on one window washer and made an appointment for him to come to our home. As it turned out, this man was a Christian, so I asked him all kinds of questions about window cleaning. He showed me how he conducted his business; so that day for the first time, I held a squeegee in my hand. Washing windows at my own home was the beginning of a six-month journey in the fall of 1997 that focused on research, prayer and practical preparation.

About three weeks later after my initial thought, I had another unusual encounter with the prompting of the Holy Spirit as I prayed in a hotel room in Houston. I was in Texas to emcee a Network for Life conference, where prison supporters and ex-prisoners gathered for networking and support.

At 6:30 a.m. I awoke and got on my knees by the bed. I began to worship the Lord and asked Him to guide my day. I always looked forward to a few moments of solitude in my hotel room as I traveled and today was not an exception. In the stillness of my mind, a thought came to me: "Get up and look out the window."

I felt a little foolish acting on the thought, but since no one was around, I did it anyway. As I pulled back the curtain on my fourth floor hotel room, I looked six stories up at the downtown building across the street. I saw two silhouetted stick figures, high above me, carefully washing windows in the early morning sun. I sat in a chair in the hotel room and began watching these men. The same unseen Presence that I felt when I was a young prisoner came again and filled the room and I began to weep. I knew God was calling me to start a window cleaning company. It was a crazy thought, but it was real.

Back home, however, the idea wasn't resonating with Jane. She felt insecure. Let's face it, she thought I was nuts. I could understand how she felt. I would be leaving a good job with Prison Fellowship, one that had provided for all our needs for many years. We had excellent benefits and health care, which was important to both of us considering Jane's MS.

As a Prison Fellowship worker in a variety of positions, I had been known as an innovator and visionary within the organization. The thought of starting my own business, without any capital or experience, was pretty far-fetched. But God's ways are not our ways, and His thoughts are not our thoughts.

"What will we do if you step out in faith?" Jane asked me as she cried one night. I was scared, too. The questions she asked me were fair and realistic; I wanted to make sure I was doing the right thing, too. I didn't have the money to start a company and I didn't know how I would find resources.

Fast forward to a couple weeks later. Jane and I were driving home from church on Sunday when I told her I thought God was calling me into a fast.

Fasting was not something I had done much of after I had become a Christian. While I had fasted only occasionally, this time felt different. After making arrangements not to work for a few days, I began my fast that Sunday with my Bible in hand and a pad of paper.

Monday afternoon, that same unseen Presence, the Holy Spirit of God, came upon me with a tingling and warmth running through my body. A still small voice inside my heart said, "I have called you to run a national window cleaning business for Me." Weeping for almost thirty minutes, I lay there and then went to Jane. It was an emotional moment for me; I could hardly talk. She cried and said she had never seen me in a state like this since we had been married.

"God will show us His will. I believe Him for that," I told her. "And I will wait for Him to show us."

Dave Manley, a very good friend of mine and an ex-convict who left prison and began to work in the field of prison ministry, was in the office with me that next Tuesday morning. The emotion of the message from God still stayed with me. I was overcome with my feelings and with God's power. Dave told me later it took me probably five minutes to get just a few lines out about what was happening to me.

Here's Dave's response to that day and to the

concept of Window King:

"The day Mel walked in and told me he felt God visited his home and told him to raise up a national window cleaning company, I struggled with what he was doing. When I first saw Mel weeping that day, though, I thought something had happened to Jane. But, no, this was about a new calling, something new God wanted to do to empower former prisoners so they could lead new lives and share the good news.

"The very next day, when I came to work, I had the same experience Mel was having. I could not stop boo-hooing! I could hardly talk. That was the greatest confirmation I have ever had in my life. It was then I knew God would open up the doors to make Window King real.

"Doors started opening for Mel. Signs and wonders happened around him. The presence of the Lord was so strong in his home. I could feel there was something undeniably different there. Someone came forward to help underwrite the business and help get it off the ground.

"Meanwhile, Jane did not understand what Mel was hearing. After spending time herself in prayer and listening to Mel's idea, however, she started to understand what got Mel so excited. Window King could be a great opportunity to be in a public service and to speak of the Lord to those who did not know him. Mel walked away

from Prison Fellowship, but he did not walk away from prison ministry.

"I was the first franchisee, Window King No. 1. From this really crazy beginning, God has blessed everything we have touched with Window King. I thank the Lord for the opportunity to be part of this."

In September 1997, I contacted my attorney and set up the company Window King. We federally trademarked our name throughout the United States. I bought a 1998 S10 pickup truck and had professional Window King decals painted on it, so I could advertise as I drove. Armed with marketing door-hangers created to introduce the homeowner to Window King, I walked the streets of Colorado Springs and Monument, Colorado. I also launched a yellow page ad and bought all the equipment I would need to clean windows.

The first house I cleaned was the home of a friend. While there, the woman next door to the house ran out of her home, yelling lightheartedly, "Oh, Window King! Oh, Window King! Will you clean my windows?" She was my second job.

From that point my business started to take off. Now into our third year, we've sold franchises to seventeen owners in eight states who themselves often choose to employ ex-prisoners. I've hired ex-cons from all backgrounds and young men who have renounced their gang affiliations and are seeking on their spiritual journey. Ten employees work with me now in Colorado from my home office.

When I clean windows, I see the task from a spiritual as well as natural point of view. A window to me represents a human life that is in pain, one that does not know Jesus Christ as Lord and Savior. Windows are people to me. I dedicate funds from the proceeds I make from Window King to reach people with the good news. The spiritual significance is that I am a vessel. I'm one of God's window cleaners. As I stand there cleaning windows, He pours his mercy, grace and compassion on me.

Window King is a vehicle to produce revenue to reach hurting men and women behind bars. I believe everything I have is from the Lord. The business is God's and I have a role in it. But it is His company and His money.

One of the most exciting parts of Window King is to see the lives that are being touched. For example, Steve, a supervisor with my company, came from a life of addiction to drugs and alcohol. Today, through the discipleship ministry within Window King, Steve married the woman he was living with, was baptized along with the rest of his family and now plays lead guitar on the worship team at his church. My greatest joy is being allowed to be part of the redemptive message and ministry of Jesus Christ, who calls us to Himself, changes our lives and turns us around to help others in need.

> *"You have made known to me the path of life; you will fill me with joy in your presence..." Psalm 16:11*

Chapter Nineteen

Pursued by His Presence

I walked back into the Nebraska State Penitentiary, not as prisoner 28138, or as an angry man. Gone was the rebellious teenager who had never experienced love. Absent was the pain that drove me to crime. The iron gates clanged shut once again. I'd been out of prison for years and was forever changed.

Flanked by security guards and the chaplain, I felt a lightness in my step that told me the Presence, that same unseen warmth of God's Spirit, was by my side. I recognized it once again. I'd felt it when was a lonely, confused, seven-year-old child sitting in an Alabama wheat field. The Presence never let go of me when I entered a cold, dusky Nebraska prison. It followed me throughout my incarceration to a small bathroom where I knelt on a cold floor and wept out my sin. The same force was there when I stood in the middle of a college classroom, wildly uncertain and mind racing about whether I was really smart enough to go back to school. And it guided me when I launched Window King with nothing more than a bucket of squeegees and a sense of a new calling in life.

I now realized that the Presence was Jesus, who walked with me in the dark places of the soul. As I stood before an auditorium of men, whose lives were so much like my old life, tears began to flow. I sensed how much Jesus loved these prisoners. His love, His compassion and His forgiveness for these men flowed through me that day out to the audience, as I shared my story of God's unseen Presence.

God's invisible concern touched me as a child and never let up. His grace kept me from killing myself. I entered a new relationship with God as I recognized I did not need to transfer my sin to Carl Scott, my youthful alias, when there was a Savior who chose to take my sin for me. It held me steady when I doubted whether I could make it outside prison.

The Spirit walked with me in the long valley of suffering as my wife slowly lost use of her arms and legs. It was God's pursuit of me, catching the attention of a broken man from a troubled past, that gave me strength to tell others about His love.

His love also invaded my family and changed us profoundly. Mother became a Christian years ago and began to pray for me while I was in prison, plus she prayed for the rest of the family. Today she lives in Omaha, Nebraska, faithfully witnessing to her faith. A year before he died, my Father asked Jesus into his heart, which gave us all great comfort.

Marlene, my oldest sister who married when I was young, has a family of five grown children and loves the Lord. Judy, the rifle-wielding sister who confronted my Mother, is married with five children. She stays active in her local church and continues to provide a leadership role in our family. Sister Jackie is married and has two grown children. She is active in outreach with her church and in ministry to people. My twin brother Marvin committed his life to Jesus years ago. He is married with four children and also active in ministry to others.

My younger sister Jan had two children, one whom is deceased, and continues to offer guidance and love to those around her. Her twin James graduated from Bible school in Tulsa, Oklahoma, in 2001 and continues to serve the Lord. James owns a Window King franchise in Tulsa. My family, in such turmoil years ago, was forever changed.

After I shared my message that day in prison,

many men pushed forward to talk to me. While the Prison Impact ministry team prayed for them, some men bowed, while other men knelt, as the chains of sin and sorrow fell away. As a former soldier in the army of the dark side, I recognized the scars of those men whose past life echoed the emptiness of drugs, depression and crime. Like these men, I had listened to the voices around me. The voices coming from within my own mind told me I was too dumb to learn anything and too slow to ever succeed. Family voices echoed that tune of defeat.

My thoughts flashed back to the moment when I stood in front of oncoming traffic, high for three days on methamphetamines. Throughout my old life I listened to the voice of Satan telling me to leave my cares and go to where there was no pain. Satan had wanted me to die. Now I knew that voice came from the depths of bondage and the master of deception himself, who blinds so many who end up in prison.

Surveying the crowd, I saw several men had a glow and a peace in their eyes showing they already had found a new life and peace. They lived for God in prison. But as I scanned the packed prison room, I saw more men carrying all kinds of burdens, the tense looks on their faces revealing shame and guilt. Hardened by the weight they carried, and living without purpose, these men had not been abandoned by God. He had made a way for their Jubilee.

My story can be your story. My hope can be yours, also. The same Jesus Christ, the Son of God, who transformed me can change you. Begin your spiritual journey to freedom with Him today. Allow Him to change your life for tomorrow.

"So if the Son sets you free, you will be free indeed." John 8:36

Chapter Twenty

Journey to Freedom

My journey to freedom took me through years of imprisonment, both behind bars and within my own history of insecurities and addictions. It took a small step of faith on my part to trust a God I could not see, to believe that He would meet me where I was, and begin the process of change.

When I began to search for God, I only saw the Christian life as one of restrictions. Would I have to lay things down, get clean from drugs or give up pleasures that had been part of my life for years? I had tried to make those lifestyle changes before and found I had no power to change myself. But once I experienced the power of His Presence, which let me know He was real, God gave me the power to become a new person.

I started seeking answers to spiritual questions

while I was in prison, and over time I began to understand God did not count my sins against me. Instead, Jesus began to give me strength to let go of those things that actually held me in bondage. God accepted me the way I was. I didn't have to change to earn His love. It was a gift freely given by Jesus' death on a cross for my salvation from sin.

My new life in Christ has been a journey of growth over twenty-five years, a process that is never fully finished until we enter the new home Christ has for us. I am tempted every day and have a choice to die to my own desires and the flesh. If I sin, the pleasure is short-lived. There are times I don't love my wife the way I should. I don't always treat employees the way Christ would have me treat them. But I do strive by the power of the Holy Spirit to be the man and the husband Jesus has called me to be. God is not done with me yet.

I would like to tell you if you commit your life to Jesus you will have no more problems. But this is not true. A commitment to Christ will cost you your life. Our old desires must continue to die and the new life must emerge each day. One way we continue the process of change is to renew our minds every day. In Romans 8:5 the Apostle Paul tells us that those who live according to their sinful nature have their mind set on what that nature desires, but those who live in line with the Spirit have their mind set on what the Spirit desires. In order to renew our mind and have it set on the Spirit, we must read the Word of God daily. We must walk this new life out one day at a time.

I come from a fatherless generation, but the Heavenly Father has been fathering me with His perfect love. There is no addiction, emotional pain or sin that can hold us captive. Jesus is able to break these bondages off our lives and by the Spirit we can lead a new life in Christ. I can't say the new life will be easy, but I can say a walk with Jesus is the only road to find true freedom.

Read the Bible each day. Commit yourself to spend time with other Christians and worship in a local church. Ask God for mentors who can walk with you in the difficult times. You will suffer troubles in this life, but rejoice that Jesus never abandons you. For though we live in this world, we do not wage war as the world does. The weapons we use to fight with are not the weapons of the world. On the contrary, they are powerful and will demolish spiritual strongholds as we take every thought captive to make it obedient to Christ. *(II Corinthians 10:3-5)*

You may have seen your own story in my life's journey to freedom. You may have asked God to touch your life before, and felt a Presence from another world touch your heart sometime during your life. Don't ignore that still small voice that speaks to your heart. Respond to the Presence of God, just like I did, to make a new start. Wholeness and healing are available in Jesus Christ.

To gain eternal life and become a new creation, invite Jesus to take authority in your life. The Bible says: *"Yet to all who received him, to those who believed in his name, he gave the right to become children of God – children born not of a natural descent, nor of human decision, or a husband's will, but born of God." John 1:12, 13*

To receive Christ means to turn your back on your old life and ways, humble yourself before God and acknowledge that your actions have turned you away from Him. Like millions of other men and women who have found new life in Christ, we all start at the same place – confessing our sins to God who made us.

Here's a sample prayer you could pray:

"God, I've gone my own way in my life. I have rebelled against You. I have made a mess of my life. Jesus, I invite you to take residence in my heart and fill me with the Holy Spirit." Amen.

And if you have known Jesus but have turned away for whatever reason from God's presence, and you would like to return, here's a simple prayer you could pray:

"God in heaven, I have not done what you have asked me to do. I have participated in

darkness and gone my own way. Please forgive me for my sin and restore me in a right relationship with you. Thank you for dying on the cross for my sins. Amen."

To better understand God's gift to you, the next step you could take is to get involved in learning and reading the Bible. Bible study is critical and will recharge your mind with truths that will change your life. Study the life of Jesus, and learn how to talk to Him through prayer. Contact your chaplain (if you are a prisoner) or a pastor in a Bible-believing church for further suggestions to help you live out your journey of faith.

Rejoice in the work God will do in you. Do not be anxious about anything, but in everything by prayer and petition, present your requests to God. And God's peace, which goes beyond all understanding, will guard your hearts and minds in Christ Jesus.

"To him who is able to keep you from falling and to present you before his glorious presence without fault and with great joy — to the only God our Savior be glory, majesty, power and authority, through Jesus Christ our Lord, before all ages, now and forevermore!" Jude 24 -25

*For more information about **Mel Goebel** and his work in prisons, contact **Prison Impact Ministries,** 590 Highway 105 #235, Monument, CO 80132-9125.*

Leading Prisoners To Christ

This edition of the 70 x 7 series /*The Unseen Presence* is provided as a free gift to reach juveniles, men and women in correctional facilities throughout the United States.

The continued success of this gift edition depends on personal contributions. **Each $1 contribution puts one book in the hands of an inmate.**

_____ **Yes, I will help!** Enclosed is my monthly contribution of $_____ to be used in leading prisoners to Christ.

Name_____
Address_____
City_____State _____Zip_____
Phone_____

Enclosed is my contribution of: $_____ to be used to provide free copies of *The Unseen Presence* (bulk copies of 72 per case)

_____ Institution Where Most Needed
_____ Specific Institution
_____ Other

Name_____
Address_____
City:_____State:_____Zip_____
Phone:_____

Prison Impact Ministries
590 Hwy. 105 #235
Monument, Colorado 80132-9125

(Prison Impact Ministries is a 501 (C) 3 non-profit organization governed by a board of directors.)

About the Authors

Mel Goebel is the owner and founder of Window King, a professional window cleaning service based in Colorado. After Mel served five years in the Nebraska State Penitentiary, he worked for the Prison Fellowship ministry for twenty years. Within Prison Fellowship organization, Mel served as state director in Colorado and Nebraska, plus he has personally ministered in hundreds of prisons and detention centers throughout the United States. Mel and his wife Jane visit men and women in prison through the work of Prison Impact Ministries out of Kalispell, Montana.

Nancy Scudder Caine is a 20-year veteran newspaper writer and editor. She lives in Cincinnati, Ohio.